LEFT-HANDED GOLF

LEFT-HANDED GOLF
by BOB CHARLES

with ROGER P. GANEM

SPORTS
PUBLISHING

Sports Publishing books may be purchased in bulk at special discounts for sales promotion, corporate gifts, fund-raising, or educational purposes. Special editions can also be created to specifications. For details, contact the Special Sales Department, Sports Publishing, 307 West 36th Street, 11th Floor, New York, NY 10018 or sportspubbooks@skyhorsepublishing.com.

Sports Publishing® is a registered trademark of Skyhorse Publishing, Inc.®, a Delaware corporation.

Visit our website at www.sportspubbooks.com.

10 9 8 7 6 5 4 3 2 1

Library of Congress Cataloging-in-Publication Data is available on file.

ISBN: 978-1-61321-347-6

Printed in the United States of America

Foreword

In the winter of 1963 I suddenly found myself in the unlikely role of a prophet. This, to be sure, was an unusual situation, but so were the facts which placed me in that position. It all concerned Bob Charles, who was making his debut on the American professional golf tour. At the time, I was one of the few in this country who knew him well. Perhaps a bit of background would best explain the minor role I have played in the Bob Charles story. He was my client long before his phenomenal success in the United States, but it was obvious to me that such success was inevitable.

Let's go back two years. As the attorney and business manager for Arnold Palmer, Jack Nicklaus, and Gary Player, I have been very close to both amateur and professional golf. This association has not been limited to the United States, as I have traveled around the world every year since 1961 carrying on various negotiations for my clients.

Toward the latter part of 1962 I accompanied Arnold to South Africa, where we were both guests of Gary Player in Johannesburg. This proved to be quite an eventful trip as it was the first time I had ever met Bob Charles, up to that time known primarily and quite simply as the "left-hander from New Zealand."

This being a world of coincidences, Bob had recently married a South African girl who was a friend of Gary's wife. He had come to South Africa to play their professional tour, and amazed everyone in that country with his steady performance. Except for golfers in New Zealand, Australia and South Africa, no one really knew very much about this impassive young man. He had thoroughly destroyed the DeSoto Lakes Country Club at the left-handers tournament in Florida that same year, winning the event by a lopsided margin of 17 strokes. This spectacular victory, coupled with the fact that he broke a long-standing course record at DeSoto Lakes, should have catapulted him into prominence in the United States. For some reason, no great significance was attached to his victory and the usual statement made by the average golf fan was: "He must be pretty good for a left-hander."

Actually the American golf fans could be excused for their lack of enthusiasm over Bob's initial appearance, since they had been treated over the years to a long string of supposedly fine left-handed players, none of whom ever achieved top ranking. To my knowledge only one left-hander played the tour regularly, and that was 10 to 15 years ago. He was of some interest in exhibitions and at tournaments, simply because he was a left-hander, but he never won any major tournaments and eventually stopped playing the tour altogether.

I must confess that before meeting Bob and seeing him play I might have had somewhat the same attitude. However, his feat at DeSoto Lakes was absolutely incredible to me as I had competed on that golf course in past years and knew it to be tremendously difficult. On that basis, before seeing him play, I suspected that he had to be more than a "pretty fair left-hander" and that his accomplishment was much more than a few "hot" rounds.

After meeting Bob in South Africa and watching him play two tournaments, I immediately accepted the request to become his attorney and business manager throughout the world. This brings me to the statement I made initially that I was put in the role of a prophet. I was confident of his future in my own mind. More than that, I found great satisfaction in voicing this confidence to all who would listen. At first, there were very few "believers."

You must understand that Arnold Palmer, with whom I first

became associated in the world of golf, was a well-known figure in American golfing circles before turning pro. He had won the National Amateur Championship in 1954 and though success did not come overnight, he did well as a professional before really breaking to the top in 1960.

Similarly, I represented Gary Player shortly after his amazing performance at the National Open in 1958. The attendant publicity surrounding that tournament had made Gary a familiar golfing competitor throughout the country almost overnight. No one has been surprised at his accomplishments since that time.

When Jack Nicklaus announced his intention to turn professional in 1961, nothing could have been added to his fame or accomplishments. He was easily the world's leading amateur and had already performed very well in several professional tournaments, including the U. S. Open and Masters Championships. Everyone was certain that he would become a great success on the professional tour almost immediately.

Such was not the case with Bob Charles. He had not competed in amateur tournaments in the United States, and had never participated in sufficient open tournaments to warrant much publicity. Therefore, he was not only an unknown from his record, but a man from outside the United States as well. I was probably one of a handful of people in the United States who even knew about his intentions to compete on the professional circuit. Those of us who did know Bob, however, including Gary and Arnold, were certain that it was only a question of time before he achieved a top ranking as a professional.

Beginning with the California tournaments in 1963, many persons were curious about this left-hander from New Zealand and I could see that most of them did not take me seriously when I stated unequivocally that he would be the first left-hander to win an American PGA tournament. People laughed when I said he had an excellent chance of winning one of the four "major" tournaments as well. Some so-called experts even intimated that I was probably a little bit out of my mind.

Bob did not make his debut until the latter part of February when the tour moved to the southeastern part of this country. By this time, everyone awaited his arrival with great curiosity. While he played steadily, it took him a little time to get used to the problems of the circuit. With a different tournament each week, there is not much time to become acquainted with each course. The greens, climate, and terrain are all different. Traveling constantly and living out of a suitcase are not particularly conducive to golf—at least until the routine becomes familiar.

The skepticism began to subside as Bob's performance improved each week. To top it off, he absolutely astounded the golfing world by winning the Houston Open in May, only three months after being on the tour, and the first of the left-handed breed to win such a tournament. It was with great satisfaction that I could finally say to all the skeptics: "I told you so!"

A few persons still maintained that it was a freak—a lucky victory. They have long since changed their tune. He is now an established player of top rank throughout the world, and is just beginning on what will continue to be a phenomenal career. I can say quite honestly that I was not at all surprised by either Houston or the British Open. After watching and associating with the greatest golfers on the tour, you become aware of the traits which are absolutely necessary to a champion.

Bob has all the tools. He is without question one of the great competitors of our time. He is ruthlessly cold-blooded on a golf course. Behind his impassive countenance is an uncompromising desire to defeat all opponents, and to destroy a golf course in the only way he knows—to break par by as many strokes as possible.

Experts say he is not long enough off the tee, but I have seen him reach a 588-yard par-5 hole with a drive and a 4-wood on a wet golf course. I have also seen him outdrive some of America's longest hitters, and even more important, he is usually straight down the middle.

As a putter he is without equal. In my judgment he has as good a putting stroke as I have ever seen and I would not be at all surprised to see him tour a golf course some day with only 18 putts. But most important of all is his temperament. He is a man of great self-discipline and plays golf as it should be played. That is, he thinks about each shot as it comes. He could miss a 6-inch putt and look no different than if he had holed out from a sand trap.

Some people say he lacks color, probably because he does not exuberantly throw his golf club, hat, or ball after executing a fine shot. There may be some people who think such shows of emotion are a necessary part of a fine golfer. I happen to disagree. Any man who can win golf tournaments in today's competition, including the British Open, needs no more color. I am happy to see him hit the ball from tee to green and play the game as he knows best.

By and large, the world of sports is an evolutionary process. That is, each athletic activity, whether it is baseball, football, golf, or what have you, is subject only to gradual change. There may be improvement in technique and there will always be outstanding performances by great athletes. However, it is seldom that drastic changes take place in any sport.

One such change which did take place, and which comes to mind quickly, is the development of the forward pass in football. Another might be the use of a fiberglass pole in pole vaulting. Still another might be the 24-second rule in professional basketball. However, the actual performers in these sports did not make the changes themselves.

One of the more recent revolutionaries in the world of sports would have to be Roger Bannister. He brought to trackmen not just a 4-minute mile, but a completely different technique of training and of driving the human body to limits which, until then, were thought impossible.

Bob Charles is perhaps the greatest revolutionary of them all. In less than one year, he succeeded in changing one philosophy of golf, which had been a rule of thumb for a hundred years. The rule was quite simple—a left-hander can never become a championship golfer.

Down through the years, golf has witnessed some truly spectacular performances, and there will always be great players who dominate the field. Bob Charles did much more than simply become one of the great players. He "broke the golf barrier" for the left-hander. In no other sport was a man handicapped because he learned to do things with his left hand. As a matter of fact, in some sports the so-called "southpaw" actually had an advantage.

Not so in golf. The youngster with a blooming golf career, even though trained to do everything else with his left hand, would receive stern advice to learn with right-handed clubs or forget about a golfing career. A good left-handed player, regardless of handicap, was always considered as something of a freak on the golf course.

Enter Bob Charles and all the myths, wives' tales, and rules against the left-hander were exploded with absolute finality in the British Open of 1963. Bob accomplished much more at Royal Lytham and St. Anne's than to win a tournament and upset a field which included all the world's great players. He established once and for all that the minority group of left-handed players could compete on even terms with their right-handed brethren. This victory was the culmination of a fantastic rise to the top of professional golf, which took less than six months.

Few golfing articles have pleased me more than a story in *Sports Illustrated*, in the issue of July 22, 1963, describing Bob's victory at the Open. The article began:

> Royal Lytham and St. Anne's, the site of the 103rd British Open, is a lean and dour golf links whose fairways thread their narrow green way between the shallow coastal sand dunes that mark the countryside of Lancashire in northern England. There last week a pair of much glorified Americans ran into some inglorious difficulties, a playoff developed between two of the most dissimiliar people ever to confront each other face to face in any sport, and the new champion turned out to be a man whose looks and personality matched the golf course itself, lean and dour Bob Charles of New Zealand.

The author of this article then described the clowning antics of Phil Rodgers, the man with whom Bob played in the 36-hole playoff, described the golf course, and then remarked about the British galleries:

> They knew how to react to Charles. Somber as an Alp and hardly more talkative, he showed his followers the kind of implacable golf and unchangeable mien that the British had not seen since Ben Hogan won their Open by four strokes in 1953. They had called Hogan the "Wee Ice Mon" and loved him as one of their own. Now here came Charles, who really was one of their own, assuming one is willing to take the British view that New Zealand is as much a part of the homeland as Piccadilly.

The article continued by describing the difficulties all the great players had with the golf course, and also described the final few holes of regular play which led to the tie and the subsequent playoff. After building a margin of five strokes, Bob ran into some difficulty, took some penalty strokes, and Rodgers came to within one stroke by some excellent play of his own. Bob was up to the challenge:

> Then on the 8th hole of the afternoon round, Charles broke Rodgers' last challenge. First, Rodgers rolled in a downhill 50-foot birdie putt and cakewalked ecstatically around the green. Amazingly, Charles stroked in a 30-foot birdie putt of his own. With no more than a flicker of a smile on his face he turned and walked off to the next tee, leaving his caddie to retrieve the ball and Rodgers to try to retrieve his shaken spirit. The caddie got the ball, but Rodgers never got back his composure. While Phil fumed, Charles continued to play impassive, almost flawless golf. He won the gallery over with his efficient dignity, and he won the playoff 140 to 148.

The final words of the article probably have more to say about Bob as a person and his golf than anything I have ever read:

> "I really have to offer my condolences to Phil," said Charles at the presentation ceremony. "I think I just demoralized him with my putter. I hate to think how many putts I sank. It is a shame we can't be joint holders of the trophy." Demoralize is a fair word for what he did to Rodgers. So is slaughter.
> "People are going to like Charles over here," said three-time British Open champion Henry Cotton after it was all over. "He plays golf in the British manner. No clowning, no exuberant gestures, no exorbitant facial expressions. It is quite possible he may even make a hero of himself, like Hogan, just by the efficient way he plays."
> To left-handers, at least, he has already made a hero of himself.

It takes something special to be a good teacher as well as performer. I know many fine players today who have no aptitude whatsoever for teaching the game. They are either uninterested, or simply unable to communicate with anyone other than a fellow professional about the basic fundamentals of the game. This is not the case with Bob Charles. I think if he wanted to quit the game today, he would easily become one of the world's finest teachers overnight. He has made a meticulous study of fundamentals and teaches in the same manner. I like to think I play a pretty good game of golf for an amateur and still maintain a "scratch" handicap. If anything goes wrong with my game, Bob can spot it immediately and I have seen him do the same thing with any number of fellow professionals.

I cannot adequately express the respect I hold for this man. He is a student, competitor, and performer of the finest rank. Above all, he is a gentleman.

I have read these pages of instruction and would not change one word. Bob spent many hours recommending changes in the diagrams, and this book reads exactly as if he were standing on the practice tee giving you a lesson. Listen to what he says about the game. It comes from a man who knows his business.

Mark H. McCormack
Cleveland, Ohio
August 24, 1964

Contents

1

The Making of a Professional

I could count many years, many tournaments and many miles from this time I first began to play golf and the moment I was getting ready to tee off on the 21st hole of the 1963 playoff for the British Open Championship. At that spot in the match I had a five stroke advantage, it thus being obvious that it was one of my good days, especially on the greens, and one of Phil Rodger's bad ones. All the things I had done to my swing to get it to reliably react to tournament pressure were working rather well for me; yet, at that precise moment I decided to put aside the driver and play a safe, sane shot with a three-wood.

The third hole at Lytham-St. Anne's plays shorter than the measured 456 yards it is from tee to green, and a decent drive would leave no more than an eight iron to get home. Although I had put one ball out of bounds in a previous round, that was with my second shot from a bunker. Now, a three-wood seemed the sensible choice, especially since I had learned that it is one thing to know how to hit the ball, another to know how to think your way around the course. However, something happened to my simple and correct swing and I hooked the ball into the British Railways. I sent the ball out of bounds *while playing it safe!*

1

Golfers are always striving for perfection out on the course, in thought and in performance. I am no exception to this trait, and I am going to assume you are not, either. The reason is obvious: Once you have developed what to you is the "perfect" swing, one that can be repeated time after time, you are going to hit all good shots. Or, to be more realistic, during any given round, you will begin hitting fewer bad shots. The strain of inconsistency will disappear and your game will improve.

Hitting the ball correctly is relatively simple. To develop a good repeating swing, you need concentrate only on timing and balance and rhythm. On paper, this *is* simple. However, in the pursuit of pleasure while playing golf, whether for fun or funds, the human element comes into it all the time, and this complicated the best of methods.

Everyone who plays is going to have some days that are much better than others. Those days when your timing and rhythm are not functioning are going to be black days when your playing suffers, but when these important elements of the golf swing are under control, your all-around play will be good.

This is no phenomenon, of course. It is quite natural, really, that your whole body, or system, will not always function as well as it should, and you're going to go through some days feeling worse than others. So it is with your golf swing. Every golfer goes through certain periods of doing things like hooking or slicing, or even both. Every so often a little change, although an unintentional one, creeps into the swing and for a time you can do nothing but slice. Then another quirk takes over and for days or weeks you might be hooking the ball. Occasionally it is difficult to make the necessary corrections and the errors might last a considerable length of time, especially among weekend golfers, too many of whom attempt to make corrections without any competent outside help. So common is this tendency that we'll devote a separate chapter to lessons.

However, if you have a golf swing that is simple *and* correct, you're going to have more good rounds and fewer bad ones than anybody else. And this means a lower handicap than the great majority.

In my younger days, going back to when I was about 17, I hit the ball very straight off the tees, my iron shots were generally fairly accurate, but I was a short hitter. I had no great length and my game was really built around chipping and putting. Yet my all-around play was reasonably consistent enough to enable me to score in the low seventies from that time until 1960 when I was 25 and I turned pro. However, just prior to and shortly after becoming a professional, I developed a tendency to duckhook the ball and, although I did gain considerably more yardage with the ball that spun in this left to right direction, particularly off the tee, I ran into a lot of trouble, as would anyone with this problem. It resulted, as I found out none too soon, when I hit from the top, starting the downswing more with my left hand rather than the right. Instead of pulling the club down with the right hand, I'd start to hit from the top with my left, thereby bringing the clubhead in too quickly. The left would overpower the right to such an extent that there'd be a quick roll over on the wrists at impact; the right wrist would break and the left would take over. This gave the ball considerable hook spin, and it would go straight about 150 yards down the center then would shoot sharply to the right.

In fighting to rid myself of this duckhook, I developed a slight fade and, believe it or not, I started to get more distance. This sounds like an impossibility and it would be in the respect that a fade will cut down on the amount of roll a ball gets after hitting the fairway. But as this was taking place, starting to control the tee shot, that is, I was also developing my golfing muscles through daily play, most of it under the pressure of tournaments just about every week of the year, and the added length came naturally.

I've retained that fade which I now play for because I like to get just a little bit of movement from right to- left. In my opinion it is a more consistent shot; you can keep it under control better, and, when things do go wrong, it then becomes easier to get out of trouble that's on the left hand side of the fairways than from the right. At least, you will then be able to keep your feet on the mowed ground while hitting your recovery shot, always a better prospect than having to go back into the trees or bushes. This is a small point, of course, but it isn't *untrue*, is it?

Four Steps to Consistency That remark about preferring rough that is on the left side of the fairway to the rough that is on the opposite side clearly shows that my game was so erratic that I had to become well acquainted with golf's many little problems, but the ball began travelling in a more direct line, that is, I was able to get control I was usually able to count on, by doing a few certain things to my swing. One, I use a fairly short backswing. Two, I keep that right arm straight. Three, I keep that left elbow tucked in as close to my side through the swing as is comfortably possible, quite close as I'm coming into the ball. Last, I don't make a big weight shift or weight change on my backswing; yet, there's quite a thrust forward on my downswing and follow-through. (It will be noticed that I have a fairly upright swing which is, I feel, only natural for a tall person such as myself.)

To guide me into a proper weight shift and to help maintain balance, my right heel stays on the ground. I think it is an unnecessary movement to lift the right heel off the ground on the backswing. Because of this, my right knee does not turn in toward the ball or flex and point behind the ball as much as it does for a lot of other golfers; my right knee, more or less, bends and points straight out, a normal movement to ease a shoulder turn for those of us with long legs and relatively short torsos.

The downswing, I feel, is started by a succession of movements, rather than by any one thing in particular. I strive for the late hit and work to get the clubhead to stay behind the hands. The "release" at the ball is the maneuver that gives me distance. Then I like to feel myself finish with a long, high follow through, because when I'm swinging the club well and finish high, I've hit the shot as well as I know how.

Using the Square Approach I do not use or encourage any wrist break, or pronation; instead, I endeavor to keep the clubface as square as possible throughout the swing. This is the approach credited to American golfers, and I think this might be true, although fine golfers in other lands were swinging similarly for the same reasons: There is less that can go wrong with the swing that must see the clubface, at impact, square to the hole. It doesn't matter whether you are a right-hander playing left-handed, as I, or a left-hander playing right-handed, as Phil Rodgers, or a left-hander playing left-handed, as most of my friends who belong to the National Association of Left-Handed Golfers, the sport of golf rewards those who built their game on squares: Everything, from top to bottom, is square to the hole and, while a variation or two may develop for one reason or other, the end result should mean that at least the clubface will be square at the time of the hit, ensuring a straight shot of the intended length.

Nothing more is needed, nothing more is required, whether you are tall, small, round, thin, young, old, male or female, an upright swinger or one who swings flat. It is true: If you were to study the swings of the professionals practicing before a tournament, or anywhere else they might be gathered, you would notice as many different swings as swingers. Each, it seems, has his own method of stance, grip, backswing, downswing and follow through. The "styles" are different, sometimes vastly so. But, in the important "impact zone," that area between the left (right for them) hip and a spot about a foot beyond the ball, most of them are precisely the same, and they come into the ball with the clubhead under excellent control—the grip, despite its variations with each performer, remains in place and firm, and the acceleration is, at that point, reaching its maximum peak. The clubface? It is *still* square to the line of flight, usually.

This is the elusive combination that, once it becomes a part of your ritual, carries you through a steadily decreasing handicap and on to bigger and better prizes.

The World's Luckiest Left-Hander There isn't a luckier left-handed golfer in the world, and I'm saying this for more reasons than my having been the first southpaw to win the British Open, an American PGA tournament, a British tournament, and have represented my country in the two big international events, the Eisenhower as an amateur and the Canada Cup for professionals. For one thing, I was born in New Zealand which boasts more left-handers per capita than any other country. Then, there is a big interest in golf there. Furthermore, my father not only liked and knew golf, but was able to teach it to me, and early in life I read every available book on golf that reached our island of more than 2,500,000 population.

Golf started for me in the cradle, literally and figuratively. You see, my mother played on a course in a town where my dad was a school teacher. We lived in a country village and my mother, unable to get a baby sitter, would take me out on the golf course in a pram. She would wheel me about while playing a round of golf and thus it was I started my golfing career in the cradle. Technically, there are photographs showing I had a golf club in my hand at the age of two, but I didn't actually begin by hitting those hard, small golf balls. I started with *tennis* balls. They were easier to contact and were less likely to break windows around the house. And that first thought, of their being easier to hit than golf balls, was my own, and in this regard, at least, my viewpoint hasn't changed.

I was encouraged to play most sports by my parents. They often bought me birthday and Christmas presents of tennis equipment, cricket bats and balls and golf clubs and, by age 15, I had my first complete set of clubs. But, prior to that, I used old clubs discarded by my parents, some of which were cut down for me. The first two clubs I started playing with were a wooden shafted mid iron (two-iron) and a mashie (five-iron). Then I was given a brassie and later a putter and thus was able to play a complete round of golf.

My First Taste of Competition   I entered my first competition when I was an unsure 16-year-old, but when I finished in the runner-up spot, my confidence developed. A year later I won my first match play victory by a narrow one-up margin, and suddenly realized that I was one of the leading amateurs in the country. This awareness does something for a fellow. (We play in the winter season at home and it gets dark at 5:30 p.m. so by the time you finish work, there is no chance to play but on weekends.) At age 18, I won the New Zealand Open with a 280, finishing ahead of Bruce Crampton by two shots and Peter Thomson by four. Although I finished runner-up in a match play event which is conducted concurrent with the Open, the members of the press started writing about me, generously calling me the best golfer in New Zealand, which further bolstered my confidence.

In 1956, when I was 20, I made my first trip overseas, travelling with another golfer to play in two tournaments in Australia. Gary Player took top honors in one of those events which also featured George Bayer and Bo Wininger. I didn't play too well but didn't worry about it: I was getting the taste of solid competition and feeling the many moods of pressure. No one had to tell me I was short off the tees and that I had to increase length if ever I hoped to amount to something. In the same year I was runner-up in the New Zealand Open and the Amateur, as well, and I represented New Zealand in a match against Australia.

In 1957 I won the Penfold Tournament and the following year left home with a friend and his wife for a seven months tour. I visited the United States and participated in such events as the Phoenix Open, St. Petersburg Open, the Masters tournament, recrossed the ocean for the British Open and British Amateur, and returned home in September. Later I played in the Eisenhower Cup matches at St. Andrews, Scotland, won by Australia in a playoff with the United States team. We finished fourth behind Great Britain-Ireland. All told, I spent 9 months overseas in 1958 and, needless to say, I gained valuable experience in just about the only way a man could if his game is to develop. Again, however, I realized that the weakest part of my game was lack of distance, being as much as 30 yards behind my playing partners; however, the rest of the game was quite good enough.

In 1959 I again won the Penfold event and represented New Zealand in the Commonwealth tournament and I visited South Africa where, among other notable occurrences, I met my wife-to-be, Verity Aldridge. In 1960, I played in my second Eisenhower Cup matches, this time held at Merion Golf Club, in Ardmore, near Philadelphia, Pennsylvania, the time Jack Nicklaus tore the course apart. When I returned home in October, I turned professional.

Actually, I had my choice of returning to work in the bank in my home town of Christchurch, or playing golf, but I had done some travelling to far away places, competed with and met some of the finest people in the world, and, since the sport of golf already had me hooked (pardon the expression) I didn't hesitate too long: I chose golf.

I thought it would take five years for me to reach my peak and make a good living, and I was prepared to turn back if, after that time, I wasn't successful. For my first trip I had $1,000 in my pocket and a round-the-world plane ticket. But I was lucky, enjoying immediate success soon after arriving in South Africa. In the first two months, I played in five tournaments and placed in the money in all of them, coming very close to winning the Dunlop Masters, coming in ahead of Harold Henning by two and Bobby Locke by four strokes. I was helped by not having a single three-putt green and dropped only three shots to par in the 72 holes on a course that measured 7,000 yards in length.

In the Western Province Open I shot 294, for a 10th place tie with Bobby Locke, then a 286 in the Transvaal Open, good enough for 3rd, two behind the winner, and another 3rd with 282 in the East Rand Open. I also played in the Natal Open, coming in 7th with a 289.

Why did I make South Africa my first stop after turning professional? Verity lived there. I had also made other friends while there previously, including George Blumberg who got me my first contract. I was able to cut expenses by staying with George and Bienda Blumberg, and in April, 1961, I went to Great Britain, followed the full European schedule, won the Bowmaker Pro-Am with a pair of 66's and led all qualifiers for the British Open with a 136 total for my only showings of note. I returned to New Zealand in September with more money than I left with, and with more confidence for the next year.

I played in the Far East Circuit in 1962, a year destined to be a memorable one, and finished 4th in overall total points to earn extra money for this designation. Then to the United States and the first Annual Doral Open, where I promptly missed the cut. But then things took a turn for the better, and in Wilmington, South Carolina, I earned about $400, then received $700 at the Masters, $350 at Greensboro, North Carolina, and left for Great Britain for the full European season.

I played good golf and won the Daks, Swiss Open, St. Moritz Open, tied for the Woodlawn Open, finished 5th in the British Open, went on to New Zealand and won a Caltex event, then placed third in the Australian Open, participated in the Canada Cup matches in Buenos Aires, then flew to the United States to play in the National Association of Left-Handed Golfers Open, winning this event at DeSoto Lakes, Florida. I quickly flew to South Africa, played in the Transvaal Open, placed second to Gary Player, and married Verity.

Now, before resuming with our golf instruction, let me pause briefly for a honeymoon. I'll do the driving and take care of the grips. Ready?

2

The Grip
Controls the Swing

The golf ball is hit with the head of the golf club which you are holding in your hands. This hitting surface can be anywhere from about 30 inches from your fingers to 44 inches or more, depending on the particular club in question. The *way* or manner in which the ball leaves the clubface on the one end depends, in a large measure, on the way you are gripping the club on the other end. So important is it in controlling the club that should you make a minor adjustment, or should the grip that is correct for your build, arm length, age and type of play be altered slightly, knowingly or not, a change in swing plane or a miss-hit might result. The moving of both hands to either side can produce a slice, hook, a low hit ball or a lofty shot. The hands of a professional or good amateur once positioned on the club do not vary, however, and if either wants to deliberately hook or slice, he would be more inclined to change his stance.

You must remember, though, that there's a great difference between golfers playing for a living and golfers playing for pleasure. I don't mean to say that the touring pros don't enjoy their work, to the contrary. But the professionals have to be able to control the ball a little better; they *have* to know how to maneuver the ball to the most advantageous spots to the best of their abilities, and it is the grip, the only contact they have with their club, that gives them this control.

Lefties Play the Same Game   In my own game, it might be said I differ from others in my grip, stance, address position, length of backswing, trajectory of shots and body turn. But I hope you notice that nowhere among the differences is the fact that I play left-handed. This is an intentional omission because I see nothing wrong with hitting the ball "from the wrong side." I have not found the strategy of play any different, or the physical exertion increased, or the mechanics of the swing any harder to master. An occasional hole may be more difficult, like the 13th at Augusta National, which is a long dog-leg left, a par-five that could be reached in two if one's tee shot is long and properly placed. This means it is made to order for a right-hander who can draw or hook his tee shot into position, whereas a right-to-left spin on any ball from me would *sacrifice*, not add, distance. This is because a ball that fades has neither the air distance nor the added roll that a controlled draw or hook has.

Generally, however, the courses are not any tougher, the number of traps and bunkers is the same, and they usually construct hazards to guard the green according to the shot required and not the person playing the hole. The size of the fairways is the same, the distances from tee to hole are the same, the cup is the same, the Rules of Golf are the same and the etiquette of play is the same. To move when a partner or opponent is putting, or to make any disconcerting noise is just as offensive when done by a left-hander as by those fellows who go about hitting the golf ball all wrong from the "other" side.

No, I cannot see anything odd about my playing the game left-handed. In fact, it is "natural" for me to hit the ball this way, and the truth of the matter is that I am otherwise a right-hander. The only time I do things as a southpaw would is when I hold an object with both hands, such as a baseball bat or cricket bat and a golf club.

My Long-Thumb Grip   I say all this to introduce my grip which *is* a bit unusual. With my right hand I more or less shake hands with the club, gripping it in such a way that I can see between two and three knuckles of the right, but the right thumb is extended down the top of the shaft in what is called the long

The Long-Thumb Grip

The most unusual part of my game is not the fact that I play left-handed: I would say it is my "long-thumb" grip. Actually, it is only a slight variation of the Vardon over-lapping grip. At the start, with my right, I shake hands with the club, gripping it predominately in the palm and in such a way that I can see between two and three knuckles, but the right thumb is extended straight down the top. By keeping the thumb under the shaft at the top of the swing, I am able to check any tendency to over-swing. This also helps me to stay in control of the club at the top of the swing where it is most important to do so.

The left hand grips the club completely with fingers-only and the pocket formed between the left thumb and the palm fits on top of the right thumb, and the little finger is crooked around the middle joint of the forefinger of the right. Thus the two hands are solidified into one strong unit that keeps the club in the proper plane and the clubface in the correct angle for power and accuracy.

The back of the right is facing the target and the left is positioned to form the "V" between the thumb and forefinger, and this "V" points upwards toward the chin. The two hands work as one, there is no slippage or strain and the "feel" of the swing is transmitted through the body into the fingers. When the hands, at impact, are as they were at address, you can be sure that the clubface will be square to the ball and a good hit will result, every time.

thumb. This gives me more control over the club nearer the top of the swing where it is more important. It definitely shortens my backswing, but this is desirable in setting up the downswing according to my way of playing. I am six foot one and a half inches tall, I'm thin and I perhaps stand closer to the ball than a shorter person would; therefore, I have an upright swing and the long thumb keeps it in the right arc for me.

In the takeaway, I come straight back off the ball (possibly you may have the impression that I'm coming outside the line, but this would be impossible unless the hands are taken out and away) into my very upright, three-quarter backswing. I also have a high follow through; consequently, it is of prime importance to keep the plane of the swing the same in the backswing and in the downswing. My grip fits this need, too.

I am also a great believer in the straight right arm at the top of the swing. Here, again, this grip serves me. Then, too, I do not let the right heel get off the ground at all, because it is not needed to get sufficient turn. Lastly, the more limited the back-swing, the less chance to overswing, too common an error, and lose control of the clubhead. The grip, especially the long thumb, keeps my hands and arms in the right place and my swing in the correct plane.

No Two Grips Are Quite Alike   In gripping the club with the long thumb, there is no noticeable "V" between the thumb and the index finger of the right hand ordinarily formed by the advocates of the short thumb method. The short thumb might be the correct grip for you, and if you find that this is so and you employ it, keep the "V" of both the right and left hands aligned and pointing upwards toward the chin or left shoulder. However, with the short thumb, I feel that the golfer will be holding the club more in the fingers, which have been known to experience a change in "feel" from day to day, and with so much more room for error, the result must be more difficult in controlling the clubhead. One of golf's most common faults is losing control of the clubhead at the top of the swing, and one of the chief causes is the fingers-only grip, referred to as the piccolo grip because of the looseness at the top. If the club is held more in the *palm* of the right hand and in the *fingers* of the left, the grip will stay firm all the way through.

With the right hand shaking hands with the club, the left is placed on the club in such a way as to allow the pocket formed between the left thumb and the palm to fit on top of the right thumb. The back of the right hand is now facing the target, and the left hand is positioned to form the "V" between the thumb and forefinger, pointing upwards toward the chin.

I use the Vardon grip which is favored by the majority of the golfers on the tour. It is also known as the overlapping grip because the little finger of the left supposedly overlaps the forefinger of the right. Actually, however, my little finger is hooked between the index finger and the middle finger of the right. This is a minor variation and is entirely up to personal adjustment and feel. Technically, grips are somewhat like fingerprints, none is quite exactly like someone else's.

If the fingers are short, I would suggest the interlocking grip, that is, positioning the hands in the same manner as described above except to interlock the little finger of the left hand with the forefinger of the right. Similarly, those with weak hands might be better off using the full-fingered grip, ofttimes called, and incorrectly so, the baseball grip. The true baseball grip is a palm grip entirely, with both hands, while in golf only the palm of the right and the fingers of the left hand would be gripping the club.

Variations of the Grip

There are only two variations of the correct golf grip; but both require the hands to function as in the Vardon: The full-fingered grip merely positions all ten fingers on the club (no over-lapping), and the interlocking grip would have the little finger of the left hand interlocked with the forefinger of the right. The majority of golfers prefer the Vardon overlapping grip; those with small or stubby fingers find the interlocking the best for their purposes and many beginners and a few outstanding professionals use the full-finger grip.

There is no particular grip that will give you extra distance. Experiment with them all, then select the one most suitable for you. But do not make any changes in position of the hands and fingers. The right grip is not going to be comfortable at the outset, so do not, in any event, move your hands around to make it any easier to grasp the club. No golfer ever reached his full potential with a bad grip; neither will you ever see a consistently good golfer who does not also have a good grip. Learn to swing the club in an even, full arc without any change in the grip, and you'll be on your way to a lifetime of golf enjoyment.

Since I started golfing, I have used all three styles. At first, I used the unlap or double hand grip, with all fingers of both hands on the club. This served the purpose until I was about 12 when I developed and used the interlocking grip—not only because I had small hands and short fingers, then, but also, I suspect, because my father used it. As you know, I imitated both my parents in those early days, even to starting off playing left-handed.

A lot of experience has gone by the boards since those memorable years in New Zealand, but I have made very few changes in the grip as I now have it. Occasionally I will move both hands under the club a little bit if I keep fading the ball, or, if I'm too strong and am hooking, I'd compensate by moving the hands more towards the hole, into a weaker position. These are the *only* changes I make with my grip—and they are for remedial purposes only. I do nothing with them when deliberately trying to hook or slice, as already pointed out.

Success Is in Your Hands   I would suggest you make no conscious effort to grip any harder with the right hand or with the left. No tension should occur; it is just a firm, natural position with both hands on the club in an easy, light grip. I happen to believe that you should increase the pressure of your hands *as you are making the backswing* until, at the top of your swing, you are gripping it a little firmer than you were at address. But restrain yourself so that no tension appears.

When you are standing up to the ball, preparing to initiate the swing, everything should be in a loose, comfortable position. The club will not fall from your hands, of course, but neither are you in any danger of squeezing the life out of it. And, at the top, everything firms up so you are able to swing freely and to hit the ball solidly. Positioned as you are at the top, with the hands poised to come into the hitting area in the same position they were at address, you'll *know* the ball is going to be on the line of flight you have selected as being the most advantageous for the next shot. Transmitting all power and direction through the body, shoulders, arms and hands into the fingers further emphasizes the need for the correct grip, and should it be uncomfortable for you at the beginning, do not despair, or, what is more important, do not change it to something easier. I'll repeat that: Do everything or anything *but* change the grip and, when you have experienced the "feel" of both hands guiding the club back, and controlling the speed of the swing as well as the direction of the clubhead, you'll be well on your way to the best golf you will ever play. In fact, there is no other way, if efficiency is your goal.

3

Know How You Stand

The privilege of saying one thing and doing quite another is not exclusive with parents and school teachers: It's the practice of many who play golf, too, and I'm afraid I am no exception. Here I'm going to advocate one method of assuming the stance while I actually use a slightly different one.

The Art of Alignment At address, I believe every part of your anatomy should be in a square position—the toes, knees, hips, shoulders, all should be square or, in other words, at right angles to the line of flight. Such is its importance that it ought to be cultivated, practiced, rehearsed, until it is almost automatic. It sets up all proper subsequent movements; it simplifies the swing, and it prevents other small but damaging faults from creeping into the movement and ruining the shot before it begins.

The matter of alignment procedure should be accorded a special place in any book on golf instruction, because no golfer is immune to the careless act of occasionally standing up to a ball incorrectly, thereby causing a bad shot no matter how perfectly the ball was stroked. To combat this, most golfers will make a particular ritual about alignment, but since most of it is taking place as the golfer is walking up to the ball, it goes unnoticed. The safest and surest way to line up to the shot is to check the direction from behind the ball. In this manner your direction

16

is easily and accurately dispensed with. The proper distance remaining between your ball and the green is another matter, and will be explored in another section.

Once the line has been solved, work on setting your feet square to it, then everything else should fall into place in a regular pattern, with the hips and shoulders lining themselves up automatically.

Address Sequence

Most of today's accomplished players began by using the "square method" as the basis of their game. When everything, from top to bottom, is square to the hole, as in *Figure A*, the end result should mean that the clubface at impact will also be square, a requisite for straight flight. Variations in this theory can be spotted in different performers, notably the professionals, some of whom work best from an open stance, *Figure B*, a closed stance, *Figure C*, or a combination, as I do, in *Figure D*. But most of them started with the square method. While they look different from each other at address, they are precisely alike in the important "impact zone" and the clubface comes through the ball "square" to the hole.

C

D

Figure A illustrates the square position of the toes, knees, hips and shoulders. A line drawn between the toes would parallel the line of flight. An open stance would have the same components pointing to the right of target. Pulling your right foot back from the line would open the stance as in *Figure B*. When the left foot is brought back, you are closing your stance, as in *Figure C*. When playing a deliberate slice, I change to an open stance. Note how the movement away from the ball would be restricted in an open stance by the fact that the entire left side is nearer the line. The club is forced back outside the line and returns to the ball in the same manner, slightly from the outside. This produces a right to left spin to the ball, resulting in the desired fade. To hook, then, I will close my stance by pulling the entire left side, from foot to hip to shoulder, back from the line, providing for more of a turn away from the ball. This encourages the clubhead to come back inside the line, and the same inside-out swing into the ball will create the left-to-right spin needed for the draw shot.

Figure D illustrates my personal "hybrid" address position: My feet are square to the line, but my hips and shoulders are slightly open, pointing about 20 degrees to the right of the target. While this gives the appearance of being ideally suited to produce a big slice, it doesn't, and a big reason for the resulting accuracy is my anchoring my right heel throughout the backswing. This combination for me is comfortable and reliable, and, though I occasionally come across the ball a bit too much, more often than not the ball gets maximum distance and remains in play.

Some Results of Faulty Footwork It is when such alignment is assumed to be correct that the errors show up. For example, if you inadvertently close your stance, by pulling the left toe back from an imaginary line drawn through the ball, pointing to your target, your backswing might be fuller because the left hip is out of the way, but you will have to pay the price of the right hip restricting the downward movement. When the right hip blocks the necessary movement into the ball, it is going to be more difficult to get through the shot. The result, unless you are completely locked in this position, will undoubtedly be a hook. When the side is "frozen," you can top the ball, sky the ball or even slice the ball. The proper swing calls for your getting your body to turn *through* the ball more, and your hands to guide the club *in unison with the body turn.*

Conversely, an open stance will force you into a restriction in the pivot going back, and you won't be able to use as much of the hip and shoulders in the return to the ball. Since much power is obtained by a coordinated movement of the hip and shoulders, an open stance deprives a golfer of this extra power and tends to cut down the distance. Furthermore, an open stance encourages an outside-in swing into the ball, imparting a right-to-left spin to the ball which, as any of the slicers of the world already knows, is not conducive to any extra roll, or to lower scores. The stance should open as you move to your shorter clubs, because then this restriction on the backswing and the ensuing action to the ball would be beneficial; but not when distance with accuracy is being sought.

If this has suddenly jolted you into the realization that the closed and open stance might produce a deliberate hook and slice respectively, you are thinking correctly. The former encourages an inside-out swing that, in the hands of the experienced player, can move the ball from left to right, and the latter, as already described, will allow the outside-in swing that is greatly responsible for the fade.

A note of caution here about both alignment and stance: Do not attempt to influence the direction of the flight of the ball by moving only the top part of your body. For example, to move the hips more to the right to prevent the ball from going to the left only paves the way for *more* of a fade or slice, which is what you were trying to avoid. Should a change in the direction be your intent, whether to the right or left, make a corresponding change in your stance.

My Hybrid Stance   Regarding my own stance at address, it is a hybrid, not altogether square, as I recommend for most golfers, especially those persons just developing a game, nor is it open. You may have already noticed this from pictures: My feet are squared to the line, but my hips and shoulders are slightly open, facing at an angle of possibly 20 degrees to the right of the target. This, of course, gives the appearance of a wide open address position, but it isn't. Neither does it cause a fade: A big reason is my footwork, which, in turn, is *the* reason I keep my right heel anchored throughout.

I find this combination to be comfortable, for one thing; but I also like to hit the ball from that address position because it permits me to come across the ball just a little bit. Contradictory? Perhaps, but again I must relate that there's a big difference between golfers playing for a living and those who do not have to depend on their score-making abilities to buy the groceries. Those of us who have to rely on tour earnings have to control the ball a little more than we did during our amateur days, and we have to know how to maneuver the ball more reliably. To keep the ball in play, with the maximum distance deliverable by my build, I have selected the controlled fade most of the time. I like to come across the ball a little bit and to get them up into the air.

Does hitting the ball in this manner ever get me into trouble that I'm trying to avoid? Yes, at times I find that I limit my pivot to such an extent that I come across the ball too much and slice it considerably. But now I know that to correct it, and quickly, I have to concentrate on turning, pivoting away from the ball without the body restriction that caused the error, and, since I play most of my shots off the right foot, the result will be a straighter ball.

I Play All My Shots Off My Right Heel   I position the ball just between the heel and toe of my right foot for most of my clubs from tee shot to wedge. When using the driver, I have my feet just a little wider apart than the width of my shoulders and my stance becomes narrower as the distance becomes shorter, giving the impression that the ball is actually moving back toward the center, or left, of the stance; but it is not so, not in my case, at any rate. I let the ball remain in the same relative position off the front foot and merely narrow and open, of course, the stance.

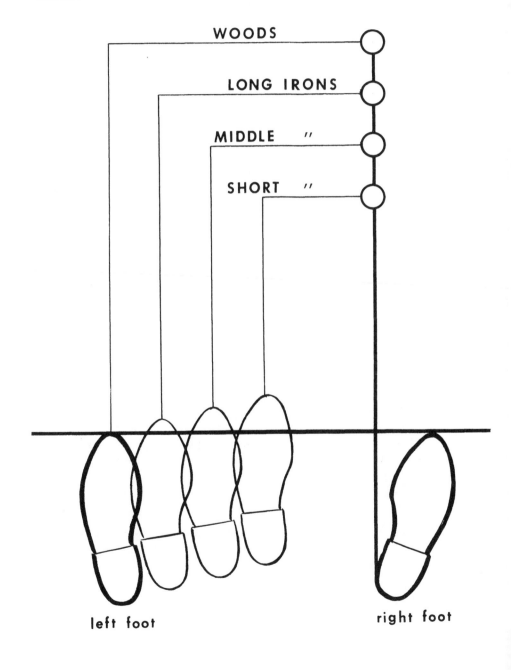

Play Ball off Right Heel

I play the ball off the right heel whether I'm using a wood or a wedge; however, as the club gets shorter in length, I open my stance and I *do* move the left foot correspondingly, so that when the stance is at its narrowest and almost open, it appears as though the ball is being played back of center. Actually there is less change in the position of the ball when hitting clubs of different length than many persons believe. To open the stance, which is helpful in hitting controlled shots, especially with the medium and short irons, you move the right foot back from the line. This moves the left side of your body more toward the target, freeing your right hip so that it doesn't get in the way of the hands which must stay on line as you are about to come into the ball and well through the hit. Thus the swing is less restricted and therefore much easier to execute. Notice what happens to the left hip when the right foot is pulled back. It acts as a deterrent for a full backswing, it limits the turn of the hip, and forces the hands to take the club back in an almost outside-in plane. Obviously, an attempt for distance from this pose would result in an uneven, strained, jerky backswing, and balance and timing would not be possible. This open stance will serve you best if it is limited to the shots you know you can execute with the club you have in your hand.

The same relative position of the ball for every club gives me the same target each time I prepare to hit. In this way there is no necessity having to adjust my body turn or change the speed or action of my hands, and my shoulders function as they are supposed to, remaining in line, as the swing continues in its even plane.

The open stance gives you a clearer picture of your target and frees the front side so that the hands move without obstruction. Do not block either the view of your target or the proper moves by trying to force the shot or by over-swinging, else you'll be defeating the purpose for opening your stance in the first place.

However, I repeat, for the golfer playing for enjoyment, I still recommend the square stance, everything square from feet to shoulders including the wrist and the forearm at the top of the swing and the clubhead throughout.

With the ball, or target, remaining constant, your entire swing, especially the plane, remains constant, also. Here, then, is where the golfer is better likely to develop that "repeating" swing that is bound to lead to more accurate, more reliable golf. The head and eyes adjust to a line that remains unchanged in relation to the direction of flight, moving in or out according to the length of the club in use; the important right arm correctly sets the

Address Stance 1

The reason why every part of your anatomy—the toes, knees, hips and shoulders—should be in a square position is that this sets up all proper subsequent moves. When everything is at right angles to the line of flight, it simplifies the swing and enables you to set a pattern for the efficient use of every club in your bag, from driver to putter, from the first move away from the ball, the take-away, body turn, top of the backswing return to the ball, impact and follow through. The square position is the only way to build a solid foundation to an efficient swing. The feet are considered to be square when the line drawn between the toes parallels the line of flight. The knees are flexed, the weight is distributed evenly, the hips are level, the body is without any tension and the head is over the ball. Because there is no tightness, no strain, the chances of your taking the club back smoothly, slowly and in the right track are in your favor, and if the start is correct, that which is to follow most likely will also be correct. As basic as this step is, it is often the predominate cause of poorly executed shots, due, sadly, to the golfer's failure to align himself up properly before he assumes his stance or from an unnecessary amount of tension even before the ball is hit.

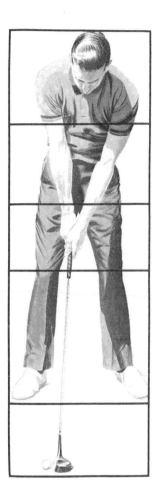

club behind the ball initially, and takes the blade into and on through in like manner for all shots, and the movement of the entire body from right to left and back to the right *in unison* with hand action and footwork becomes rhythmical. The square stance is not a difficult position to get into, it is far easier to swing and your golf will be more consistent.

4

Checkpoints Before the Hit

I don't believe there is any other game which offers as many second chances as does golf. Therefore, if you assume the attitude of never giving up, you are going to be able to score. Golf is known as being a game of recovery, and this means you always have a chance to save a stroke when you may think you're in an impossible situation. So do not let fear grip you *before you even hit the shot!*

Therefore, at the beginning, as you are standing over the ball and are about to set the machinery in motion, avoid any tension in the golf swing. It is all right for the golfer to be keyed up and perhaps a little tense prior to playing in competition. That is a natural reaction for anyone who plays a very competitive game, and it is more to be desired than a feeling of complete relaxation, which might signify that the golfer is stale, or has lost his fighting spirit. However, during the swing, especially at the beginning, you should not let any tension or tightness creep in.

Tightness often forces the over-anxious golfer to grip the club too firmly, which hinders the necessary free, easy movement of the hands and deadens the feel which is important in swinging the club. This is by no means a fault found only in the high handicapper. I had to overcome this tendency, too, and to help, I had the grips on my clubs built up thicker than standard. With my long fingers, I needed extra padding, anyway, but the larger grips also meant there was less chance of squeezing them to death. It is very wrong to think that the tighter you grip, the better feel you will have. Anxiety and tension result from this practice, and many of golf's bad shots are caused by those twin errors. Hitting the shot correctly is one of golf's most satisfying thrills, so why lessen chances of doing so by being too anxious to see the results. You might try to remember this tip which I call the four "S's." It is a formula for timing and rhythm: Swing Slow, Short and Stay down.

It is one thing to be over-anxious because you lack confidence in your ability; it is another to be too anxious because of *over-confidence!*

The Four "S" Formula   With the fear of oneself dispensed with, helped, I hope, with the four "S" formula, the next prerequisite is the blocking out of all other disconcerting elements. For example, where to play the shot. Although you may find it difficult to look continually ahead when you might be thinking of what has just happened, like the bogey or birdie you might have taken on the preceding hole, never look back. This type of thinking often blinds you to some sort of trouble that awaits your next shot, and if you are not in control of yourself, it will attract you like a magnet. Forget what might have or what actually did happen on the hole which you have just played, and concentrate on the hole or the shot with which you are faced. If you are on the first tee, about to get underway, or if you've been toiling under the hot sun for hours, you must play the next shot as a separate one altogether, and concentrate on how you are going to make your par or birdie even though things have been going badly for you.

In any type of golf, it is important that one concentrate to his fullest, each shot must be played with the sole idea of hitting it as if it were going to be the best shot you ever made; that you're going to hit as straight as you can off the tee and as straight as you can for the flag and that you are going to hole the putt. You must consider each of these shots accordingly, and separately. And where does it begin? As you are addressing the ball, getting set to put your swing into motion. Do not *hope* for a good shot. Concentrate, without undue tension, on pulling off the proper shot *through correct procedure, instead.*

5
The Key Moves of the Backswing

In starting the backswing, or the takeaway as it is often called, move the clubhead, hands and arms in one piece and at the same time, together with the shoulders turning away, so that the club is taken back straight from the ball. Get the "feel" of the clubhead in your hands, because, when you do, this important move away from the ball will become relatively simple, even for the novice. Good, consistent golf actually depends on a good move here.

The Turn Is Natural It may also be refreshing to know that you won't have to worry about becoming too stiff and "freezing" in the midst of this action, or swaying, or getting too flatfooted, resulting in your taking the club too far on that line: As the shoulders take over, you will quite naturally turn inside the line of flight, then, when the hands become waist high, the wrists start to cock, remaining that way until the top of the backswing is reached—although the actual top will depend on the length of the club you are using and your personal physical make-up. You know that I go back no more than three-quarters, but, on the average, if you were using the longest club in the bag, which is the driver, the top of your swing might be reached when your hands are above your shoulders and the shaft of the club is horizontal to the ground. As the clubs get shorter in length, the backswing likewise will be lessened.

No Pronation of Wrists Throughout this activity, the clubface and hands maintain their square position, primarily due to the absence of any rolling of the wrists, or pronating, as has been so publicized in the past. In golf parlance, pronation refers to the rolling of the wrists outward and over which results in an open clubface at the top of the swing, necessitating, of course, a return to the original position by another but reverse roll of the wrists coming down. This, I think, is a dangerous, often unreliable movement, *if* the swing is to be kept as simple as possible by reducing the number of steps which make it up. The eliminating of this one movement also results in the doing away of many others involving every part of the body.

Watch the Body Lines The angle of the arc of the takeaway depends a lot on the build of the person, and every golfer has a different plane to his swing. The plane, in effect, is the angle of the arc of your swing. The shorter a golfer is, normally, the flatter he'll swing, and the tall person, like myself, will swing in a more upright plane. The other factors influencing the arc and the clubface position are length of arms and suppleness of wrists, but, if you develop clubhead "feel" and learn to swing without any pronation of the wrists, those two elements of arms and wrists need not and should not add confusion to the requirements of hitting the golf ball long and straight.

Whether your backswing is as upright as mine, or flat, keep it the same in the backswing as on the downswing, because a swing that is too much outside the line will lead to a slice, and one that is too much on the inside will produce a hook. And, once again, if you are suddenly jolted into thinking this to be a way to deliberately hook or slice a ball, you are again thinking quite correctly. But, in developing your game, use a straight takeaway and return to the ball in the same plane.

6

What It's Like on Top

The Head Is Steady—Both Eyes Are Seeing The top of the backswing is reached when you feel a stiffening of all the muscles in your right shoulder and all along your right side. The heel does not come off the ground, the weight stays inside the left foot and your swing has balance. There will be a feeling of pressure that will make you want to turn your head away from the ball. I say resist this, if not the actual move itself, at least the tendency to do so. Build your swing around the fixed *thought* that you are not going to move your head, even though you succumb to a slight movement on the backswing. It is important that this be so, and vital that you have both eyes fixed on the ball. You must be able to see the ball with both eyes, not just one of them. In seeing the object with just one eye, you would then have turned your swing back too far and have turned away from the ball too much. But by keeping your head steady and both eyes glued on the ball, you will soon get yourself and your swing under good control.

Flex the Left Knee, Too Your right knee will turn in toward and behind the ball and your left knee must be slightly flexed, as it was at address. The slight bend given to the left knee, often unattended to, allows you to turn away from the ball smoothly, prevents a breakdown in your swing, and permits you to start

30

the downswing a little easier. If that knee were to stiffen, a jerking action would develop under the swing and there would be a loss in rhythm and effectiveness.

Wrist Position at Top of Swing

The clubface at the top of the swing must be in one of three positions: open, as in *Figure A*, square as in *Figure B*, or closed as in *Figure C*. Notice how this can be controlled by the manner in which the right wrist is positioned. The square position of *Figure B* is the one most of the playing professionals use, because it minimizes the chances of error and eliminates the need to affect a similar action on the downswing if the club is to be square to the ball at impact.

Figure C shows the left hand well under the shaft. This either encourages a flat backswing or a closed face that may result in a duck hook unless it is not allowed to further collapse during the hit. Let me hasten to say that many outstanding golfers employ this style. Similarly, many are better able to control the entire club and keep it pointed toward the target by arching the wrists as in *Figure A*. Your wrists will be positioned properly if they keep the clubhead moving in an even, efficient plane, with the hands at least up to shoulder height on the top of the backswing.

Once you have discovered how your wrists affect the backswing—and you must realize that once you have committed yourself to a "track" or line going away from the ball, you more or less have to remain on this line until the ball is hit or mis-hit, you should practice to groove this swing until it becomes automatic and then pay no more attention to them. Other than controlling the direction of the clubface, the wrists need not be concerned with, because they function best in imparting the energy to hit the ball long when they are allowed to do this vital work naturally, smoothly, almost loosely.

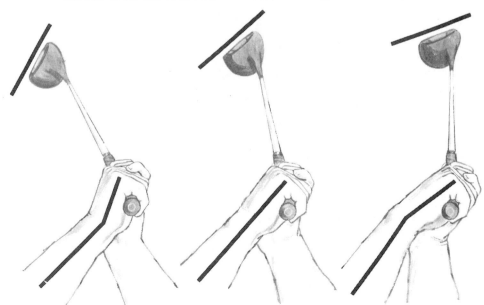

Top of Swing

At the top of the swing, the shaft of my driver is just a bit short of being horizontal to the ground. I'd be over-swinging if the shaft went beyond the point of being parallel and so would you. To guard against this common and disastrous fault, keep a firm grip on the club, especially with the last three fingers of the right hand. But as important as it is to avoid "looseness at the top," the remedy can be over-done: The lower fingers can be tightened to the extent that they bring into the swing the muscles located at the base of the forearm, rendering the wrist completely useless, and hitting the ball with the back of the right hand would be impossible. I would suggest you make no conscious effort to grip any harder with the right hand or the left. And I happen to believe that you should increase the pressure of both hands as you are making the backswing until, when you have reached the top of the swing, you are gripping it a little firmer than you were at address.

Don't do anything that will upset your timing and pull you off balance. The thumb under the shaft and the firm pressure of your grip will help keep you from overswinging; the left elbow pointing down at the ground helps keep the club in the correct plane, as do the firm wrists; the head remains fixed as the right shoulder, lower than the left, moves under the chin and the right arm is quite stiff, as stiff as you can get it. The shoulder turn is full and the back is almost at right angles to the line of flight, and the hips have turned approximately 45 degrees. The right heel does not come up off the ground, the weight is evenly distributed, the left knee has remained flexed throughout and, poised to begin the downswing smoothly, I feel some pressure on the inside of the left foot.

The Full Shoulder Turn   At the top of your swing, you'll find that your hips and shoulders are fully turned, that the back of your shoulders will almost be at right angles to the line of flight. You'll also discover that your chin is tucked into your right shoulder, and this provides a second checkpoint—the angle formed by a line running from your shoulders to the ball. At the top of the swing, your right shoulder must be lower than your left. You will also notice that your hips are at an angle of approximately 45 degrees, about half that of the shoulders, and you should find that this position will be rather comfortable.

A Straight Right Arm   I am a great believer in the straight right arm, even at the top. I never like to see anyone with that bent-over right arm, because it not only signifies some heavy, usually unnecessary muscle strains somewhere, but that the arc of the clubhead will not be consistent. Get your right arm quite straight, not exactly poker stiff, perhaps, but as straight as you can naturally get it. At least, work on getting it to feel as though it is straight.

The Left Elbow Is In   Another valuable checkpoint is the left elbow. It plays its biggest part in getting your clubhead into the ball properly, but even at this stage its value must be recognized. Tuck it in at address, and visualize how it helps keep the plane of the swing smooth, the clubhead square. Try moving it in different positions and distances from your body. It'll be well worth the experimenting. After experiencing the feeling of the elbow brushing in close, or the folly of trying to pack it in too much or, much worse, to let it fly out away from your body, you'll then know how to hit the ball. At the top, it will be a bit away from you, but still comfortably "in," generally pointing to the ground. The feeling will be of compactness; you'll be able to see, out of the corner of your eye, the smooth, full arc of the clubhead. Your swing is beginning to take on efficiency.

7

The Fact and Feel
of the Downswing

I can't say that the downswing is started by any one thing in particular. I feel, myself, that it is just a succession of movements that do it initially and, therefore, I will not emphasize any one particular factor, unless it is the hips. Now this was quite a mouthful, I realize, but I do not wish to make any issue on any difference between *fact* and *feel*.

Does the Hip Start the Action? We have all heard it said that there actually is no real top of the backswing, that the hands and club are still going back when the hips have started *their* move out of the way of the downswing. It would seem, then, that the hips truly start the move in the other direction. This may well be, as it is sometimes shown in sequence pictures, but I strive to have the hands, arms, shoulders being pulled down together. The precise flow is that of the hands being pulled down *as* the shoulders are turning and the hips sliding, with all of these movements working in coordination with each other. The objective here is not to prove what came first, the chicken or the egg, but to ask that you accept, in your own mind, whatever *particular* initial movement will get *your body and hands* in proper position to hit the ball long and consistently straight.

Develop the Late Hit If distance is to result, try for the late hit. That is, get the clubhead to always work behind the hands.

35

If the hands lead the clubhead into the hitting area, the later the hit will be, and the later the hit, the more distance. Now there are three faults that can occur here. One is too late a hit, another is hitting too early. Too early means hitting from the top, invariably caused by a rolling of the wrists as when the left hand overpowers the right coming down. The result is a hook or a pull, the ball travelling from left to right. Conversely, when you hit too late, the clubhead is delayed to such an extent that the right hand leads the left too much, there is a cutting action across the ball, and you will slice, pushing or fading the ball from right to left. The third fault? An upset in rhythm, which well might be the real culprit in the other two errors.

A

B

Release the Left Side before Hit

The downswing that is stopped just as the hands start to enter the hitting zone, *Figure A*, showing the clubhead lagging well behind, is one of golf's most grotesque pictures. But it is also one of golf's most revealing. It explains many of the game's mysterious expressions concerning centrifugal force, the late hit, lateral move of the right hip, head behind the ball, elbow brushing the hip, left shoulder staying inside and under, and the released left side.

The initial move back to the ball is not started by any one thing in particular. I feel that it is just a succession of movements. It may well be started by a lateral move of the right hip, but I do not wish to make any issue on any difference between *fact* and *feel*. The hips may well lead, but I strive to have the hands, arms, shoulders all being pulled down together. Accept for yourself whatever particular movement that will get your body and hands in proper position to hit the long ball consistently straight. But the right hip, in fact, the entire right side, has moved laterally and then it sets solidly, waiting for the hands to hit into the "stone wall," so to speak. Neither the hips nor the shoulders have turned around; rather, the hips have first started forward and the shoulders get into the shot, with the left well inside and lower than the right. The left elbow brushes in close to the left hip, both hands have remained in the same position on the club and the left side has begun to release, *all before the hands get into the hitting area.* Despite the appearance of awkwardness, the golfer is not under any strain, or he shouldn't be, and he is able to gradually and smoothly increase clubhead speed until it is at its greatest at impact, reached a split-second later. With less effort than realized, the ball is contacted with all the power of centrifugal force. The chief ingredients? Balance and timing.

Impact, *Figure B*, is truly the point of no return because as already shown, here is where the greatest clubhead speed is generated and any attempt to change the course of action would be senseless. All other components of the swing, except for the grip, have already been taken care of or should have been—by your having kept the left shoulder under and inside and the left elbow in close to the hip, and with a right arm lead, you are assured of the club's being on the correct plane. But this isn't always enough: All will be fruitless if you haven't kept your grip intact and in the same position at the time the ball is struck as it was at address when you had originally lined the club square to the line of flight.

So it is that everything about the swing is completely dependent on the correct grip, and that the flow of power is finally transmitted from the legs, body and arms into the fingers which guide the clubhead through the ball. An intense study of this pose is not necessary to see that the golf swing, while smooth, even and seemingly effortless, does call for solid if not violent, action. It is most effectively handled through balance, timing and the right grip.

The Right Arm Guides All   In the downswing, the right hand is there for the dual purpose of leading and guiding the club. The hit, itself, is applied with the left; however, you must remember that there's no conscious effort to think of either hand in particular, they must both work together, as a unit, with neither one dominating the other, causing, as you now know, a hit that is too early or too late.

Thus the right arm continues on through until almost the completion of the follow through. There will be an obvious rolling action of the left hand over the right, but that is quite natural and there should be no deliberate or disconcerting attempt to try and stop this. Instead, pay some attention to what the shoulders and left elbow must do to ensure distance with reliable accuracy: Coming into the ball, the left shoulder stays behind and goes below the level of the right shoulder until, almost at impact, the shoulders will be in a line and pointing at an angle of 30 degrees to the right of target. Check this out carefully, because this awareness will preclude any tendency to move the left shoulder *out* over the line, meaning a change will occur in the club's plane. Be certain the left elbow brushes the left hip. The shoulder will then stay inside and the plane of the swing and the squareness of the clubface will be assured. It provides another service: It will help guide your hands in a fine arc and you will be correctly swinging into and through the ball. Your swing will have compactness.

The Left Shoulder—Left Elbow Combination The hips have moved considerably and quite fast and, as you contact the ball with your tummy, so to speak, the hips will be facing at an angle of 45 degrees away from the ball. This is the time for the left elbow to stay tucked well into the side, because it is a big help in preventing the shoulders from causing a slice or even a pull by their turning away from the line. So remember, you must keep that left shoulder down and behind the ball as long as possible, and a left elbow that is in close helps more than just a little.

Release the Left Side The more efficiently you attune your swing, the more power you are going to supply and the more distance will result. Power, you know, is weight plus speed, and clubhead speed is generated through a fast movement of the hands *through the hitting area*. It is important to get everything in a correct position in that hitting area, meaning that attention must be given to your shoulders, hands, hips and feet, all of which have a part in your getting additional yardage off the tee. The rapid shift of weight on the downswing, said weight moving forward together with the maximum amount of clubhead speed possible, is what gives distance off the tee. This, plus, perhaps, a kicking action with the left foot, taking all the weight off the left and moving it up into your right so that it can be felt clear up through your legs and through the shoulders. From this action you'll find that your left heel lifts up off the ground, your left knee and your body have turned and you are facing the hole, and that you will rise up onto your left toe, the correct position at the completion of your swing.

The Follow-Through Just Happens   After hitting the ball, the clubhead carries on through and continues straight towards the hole, with the arms and hands likewise going straight out after the ball. There is no break in the elbows or in the wrists in the early stages of the follow-through, not until the natural roll of the left hand over the right begins to occur, and this takes place when the hands skip past at waist level. But let this take place as a result, rather than a pre-conceived maneuver, because it will. You do not have to concern yourself with it. I don't. In fact, I like to keep the clubhead square to the line as long as I can after the hit, and the right elbow is forced to bend only after I am well into my follow through.

How much time does it take to hit a golf ball? A few seconds?

Here we have gone into great detail about the whys and wherefores and are just getting around to hitting the shot! But the preparation for the shot is a real challenge which I find to be one of the great thrills of golf. It calls for the greatest of care if only because you have no one to help you execute the initial shot or to recover from the next, should too many things go wrong.

Never Over-Extend Yourself   But not too much will go wrong once you decide on how to groove your swing, developing rhythm according to your own physical endowments, and being content to hit the ball while staying within your own capabilities. It is usually when a person tries to over-extend himself that trouble enters into his game. He tries, when he shouldn't, to hit the long ball. Then, too, you recall at least one instance, my own, when the reverse, that of playing it too cozy, led to near misfortune.

Follow Through—It's a Result

Power is weight plus speed. The rapid shift of weight on the down-swing, moving forward in coordination with the maximum amount of clubhead speed possible, is what gives distance off the tee. This, plus, perhaps, a kicking action with the left foot, taking all the weight off the left (releasing this side entirely), and moving it up into your right so that it can be felt clear up through your legs and through the shoulders, means extra yardage. You'll not have to worry or wonder if your left heel lifts up off the ground, your left knee and your body have turned and you are facing the hole, that you will rise up onto your left to the correct position at the completion of the swing. You will not have to concern yourself with any of these natural movements, *if the weight at impact is off the left leg and completely on the right*. Let the right arm lead but hit the ball with *both* hands, with the left side completely "released" and the follow through, as illustrated, will take care of itself.

Sequence 1—11

The first movements of the swing, as short a distance as shown between Illustration 1 and 2, when the clubhead has moved about 12 to 15 inches, can actually be the difference between a good hit and a bad. This is where the foundation of the swing is laid, and if the start is correct and on the right track, the chances are excellent that the ensuing moves will be correct. Initially, *there is no wrist break.* To set myself so that the top of the backswing is reached without body strain, I begin with the knees flexed, feet solidly anchored, right arm stiff and head as still as possible.

1   2

3   4

In Illustration 4 the right knee begins its flex in toward the ball and in 5 the shoulder turn has become twice that of the hips. There is a feeling of solid pressure on the inside of my left foot but the right heel does not come up off the ground, and the right shoulder is under the chin. These are my checkpoints when I have reached the top of my backswing which, you'll notice, does not quite reach the horizontal.

Illustration 6 is a revealing one: While the plane of the club follows approximately the same line returning to the ball as it did

5

6

on the takeaway, the left elbow, pointing down, is ready to brush the left hip and the left shoulder stays under and inside. This returns the club to the ball from the inside-out.

The entire right side begins to firm up as the hands, in Illustrations 7 and 8, take the club across the body and into the ball. The "late hit" of which I speak in the text is another description of centrifugal force; the clubhead lags behind the hands and its weight and the force of the downward pull create the power that gives

7   8

maximum distance. While the right side remains firmly set, the left side "releases" to allow freedom of hand movement and a continued application of this centrifugal force. There is no stopping. When the left side remained set, the clubhead follows an inefficient path and most of the power, as well as accuracy, is lost or dissipated. Because the left side has moved into the shot, the hands were able to direct the clubhead through the ball in the correct line and the left shoulder was able to get into the shot, as well, staying inside and under the right.

9

After the hit, shown in Illustration 9, there is nothing else for the hands to do but to pull the body around and finish high, Illustration 10 and 11. You are seeing the first movement of the head. Both hands retain their firm hold on the club, and stay in the same position. The left never actually over-powers nor crosses over the right, which exerts the same pressure at the top of the follow-through as it did at the top of the backswing. At the finish the body is pointing toward the target, the right foot remains solidly planted and the left foot, except for the toe, is raised.

10   11

Keep the Head Behind the Hit Long hitting is achieved through weight plus speed, as previously stated, but the secret of the application of this formula is to get your golfing muscles very finely attuned to swinging a golf club. The golfer who plays only on weekends, perhaps one or two rounds of golf a week, admittedly has very little chance of developing good distance off the tee. If this is you, your game won't be developed to the maximum; however, you will be able to hit the ball a lot longer if you try your best to adhere to the following principles: Take the clubhead back in a very wide, long arc. You don't necessarily have to have a long backswing, but it ought to reach the horizontal when at the top, or close to it. From this position your hands will take over. Learn to develop clubhead speed by whipping the hands through the hitting area with that late hit we mentioned earlier. The late hit, fast hand action into and through the ball, with as much weight behind the hit as you can apply, proper use of the feet, with the hips sliding into the ball and your shoulders moving under and then around as fast as you can maneuver them, all add up to the long hit.

Another helpful ingredient for the long ball is to hit up against a very solid right side. This means that everything on the right must be as firm as you can get it at impact—your right arm, right elbow, right leg. Once the ball has been hit I, personally speaking, like to get a very high finish. I achieve this by keeping the left shoulder down and under until I feel it starting to pull my head around and up to watch the flight of the ball. (If this did not take place, chances are the head would remain down. So don't move your head voluntarily; it'll only lead to your coming up off the ball too soon.) Throughout this entire movement, I have gripped the club firmly and with both hands in place.

8

The Strategy of Club Selection

The Woods for Distance   The driver is used from the tee, as I know you know, but it ought not be automatically selected on all occasions, neither for many a weekend golfer nor the veteran professional. This club is for distance only, and if you ever feel you cannot gain sufficient accuracy with it, it is better to use another wood or even a long iron off the tee. I used the three-wood on three holes during the British Open playoff. One you already know about, but twice on the par-four 394-yard eighth I teed up with the spoon, as it is also called, and played that particular hole in one under par figures.

When using the driver, tee the ball fairly high, because it must be swept off the tee. No contact is made with the ground, giving this shot an exclusiveness of sorts: it's the only one in golf where there's no divot taken. Remember that the driver should be used only when you have plenty of room and/or are in need of a lot of distance.

Many Uses of Fairway Woods   The fairway woods consist of the number two wood, or brassie, number three wood or spoon, number four wood and number five wood, with some that feature face lofts in between these, now listed as the 2½, 3½ and 4½ woods. Of these, the brassie is the most difficult to master, and the most dangerous for the weekender to use. But it will give

49

the maximum of fairway distance, if the lie is near-perfect, and it is a club that can be used when the driver goes sour. It can propel a ball almost as long as does the driver and has about three degrees more loft. But it has become so expendable that if a professional needed to eliminate one club in order to carry two wedges and a 1-iron in his complement of 14 clubs as allowed by the rules, he would undoubtedly take out the brassie.

The predominate choice of a fairway wood under most circumstances, however, is more often the three- or four-wood. When using them, strike the ball with more of a downward, descending blow than called for with a driver. You should even take a bit of a divot, not, however, to the extent you would when using an iron. The woods are the longest clubs in your bag and consequently clubhead speed is easier to develop. Although some of them have less loft than do the long irons, because of their added length they can propel a ball in a higher trajectory, often making these clubs ideal to use to a green around 185 to 220 yards away and protected in front by a hazard, or out of some types of rough when the grass is thin enough to allow the clubhead to move through.

The five wood and the six wood, either or both of which might have to be specially ordered through your own professional, are good clubs for those who can't seem to be able to get any satisfaction out of their long irons, or by a person whose age and physical make-up might prompt him to use these rather than the irons, or by the ladies.

Iron Address Position

I don't know how many potential holes-in-one, well, let's say "gimme" birdies, are ruined by carelessness at the address position. If your alignment is wrong, your direction will be wrong. The best place from which to sight your target is behind the ball, even as you are walking toward it. Next, place the club blade in back of the ball with the bottom edge, not the top line, at right angles to the line of flight. *Then* assume your natural stance, without any body or feet waggling or shift in hip or shoulder position. At times a golfer is inclined to move all parts of the body in an attempt to influence the direction the ball will travel except the only part which will have a bearing on his accuracy: his feet. If there is to be any last minute change, don't forget to include both feet in the maneuver.

In *Figure A*, I am playing the ball off the right heel, as I do for all the clubs; the right arm is rather poker stiff. This may be too rigid for most players and to try it may *add* tension, instead of lessening it. But by all means do all you can to at least keep that important front arm "straight." Your knees must be flexed, head over the ball, body comfortably in balance so that all subsequent moves can be made with a minimum of strain. Do not start your backswing when you are unsure. You can hit the green with every iron in your bag. Proper execution, then, calls for positive thoughts.

A

How to Hit the Long Irons Gaining in popularity because they combine distance with accuracy are the long irons, numbers one through four. Why they are avoided by the majority of golfers is hard to understand. Their lofts are, respectively, 17, 20, 23, and 27 degrees, with that of the one-iron approximating the 17½ degrees of a present-day 3½ wood. They are also shorter in length than the woods, measuring, again respectively, 39¹⁄₁₆, 38⅝, 38³⁄₁₆ and 37¾ inches. Because of this, you are standing closer to the ball, and the backswing is not as long, both of which would seem to make the long irons easier to use and preferred rather than feared.

The swing incorporates some of the features of the fairway woods, the large sweep of the clubhead and the big body turn; but the ball is hit instead with a descending blow, contact is made on the ball first and the divot taken after the hit, and the golfer should not be satisfied if he cannot hit a pre-determined target with a modest amount of regularity, even with these long-feared long irons. Besides being stroke savers, the properly stroked long iron supplies a sweet feeling not duplicated in any other grouping of clubs. Of the 59 shots I hit with clubs other than the driver during the British Open playoff, 10 of them were with the long irons, selected for distance *with* accuracy.

Top of Swing—Iron

How long does it take to hit an iron shot? A few seconds from the time you begin the takeaway? Does it take *you less* time to get to the top of your swing than it does to return to the ball? If so, you are one of many making that common error—too fast a backswing. And when it happens with the irons, it goes without saying that the results are bad. All golfers, regardless of handicap, must expect and have a large degree of accuracy from these clubs, especially from the middle irons on down, and going back too fast, or when under too much strain, will make it virtually impossible to make the solid, sure contact that is necessary for preciseness.

I have developed the feel of staying on the same line going back as I do coming down. The backswing is shortened to a degree in keeping with the particular iron I am using, and in *Figure B* I am going with a three-quarter swing for the middle iron I have in my hands. Should I need more distance than this swing will produce, I would change to a longer club. Of equal importance to a slow backswing, then, is your knowing your capabilities with each of your iron clubs, and, once you have made your selection, you can then concentrate only on the now-simplified mechanics of the swing.

B

Middle Iron Techniques The middle irons are the five, six and seven, with respective lofts of 31, 35 and 39 degrees, and lengths of 37⅚₆, 36⅞, and 36⅞₆. These clubs are precision-built for precision shotmaking, and can or rather should be used from around 160 yards down to approximately 130 yards from the green with complete confidence. Because of their higher loft and shorter length, these clubs require a shorter backswing, smaller body turn, less weight shift, and more of a downward blow. Otherwise, there is no change in rhythm and balance.

But knowing how to swing these clubs is not always enough: You must consider the type of fairway, the lie, and the weather, as well. From a tight lie, use at least one club longer than normal because, in going after the ball, you will get or put onto the ball more backswing than usual, taking away some of the distance. But if the ball is on a very fluffy lie, such as sitting on top of a lot of clover, the reverse takes place and you will get maximum distance, no backspin. A lot of roll results when you play a shot from bent grass, also. Compensate for this overspin, or lack of backspin or however you wish to account for it, by using a shorter club, because you have to expect the ball to fly out.

Hitting out of rough produces the same type of spin created when the ball rolls off the high grass. When the rough is deep, always resort to just getting out, and never try for the miracle of hitting the ball over water, under a tree and clear of a trap, just to set up a hypothetical situation. Instead, play it safe back onto the fairway and hope for a chip and one putt for your par. It happened to me this way many times, but the most memorable took place during the same British Open. The 24th hole at Royal Lytham, at 466 yards, saw my drive hook into the right rough, leaving me no other alternative but to get it safely out. I used a five-iron. Then, my recovery wedge shot stopped within 5 feet of the cup and the putt went in for a scrambling par.

The Valuable Short Irons This, then, naturally leads to the most valuable short irons, the pin-splitting eight, nine, pitching wedge and sand wedge. There might be some golfers somewhere who could get along without the wedge, but I could not, I'm sure. Almost without exception, every shot from about 100 yards into the green, including sand, rough and apron, I make with the wedge. I would have to be faced with a longer shot, around the

140 yard mark, to consider the eight-iron. I'll admit this is about the distance I would also use a seven, the club I would select only if the lie were tight, or if playing from hard ground. But I would not hit the shot firm; instead, I would concentrate on contacting the ball and hitting it crisply to produce a lot of back-spin. I would pitch this shot right up to the hole, knowing it would bite very quickly. If, however, from the same distance the ball were setting up high on a lot of grass, I would take the nine-iron and plan to hit the ball high and hard, well short of the pin, knowing it will come down and roll a bit toward the hole.

C$_1$

Impact Area (Two Views) Iron

Here are two additional views of the downswing action *stopped* just as the hands enter the hitting zone, that point between the left hip and the ball, itself. It would appear that I am in an awkward position, caused by an anxious desire to chop down on the ball, yet, none of the fluid motion of the swing is lost, and neither is the arc created by the clubhead interrupted or broken. The hands are beginning to move faster, actually are just *starting* their swinging action and will accelerate at their fastest when the clubhead is about to contact the ball. Incidentally, the hands continue this same motion on the same line through the ball, finishing high. Guiding the clubhead along the correct path are the right arm which remains straight; the left elbow which is hugging the left hip; the "release" of the left side, notably the left knee which is now free to bend in and point to the front of the ball; the firm right side, from the foot up to the shoulder; the left shoulder remaining inside the line, the moving hands, and the not-to-be-neglected basic ingredients of correct grip, timing and balance.

C_2

After Impact Iron Shot

Notice in *Figure D* the distance the hands have travelled when compared with *Figure C*, while the right side has remained firm, the right foot solidly planted, and the head quite still. Between these two points the hands have moved smoothly but quickly, absorbing the shock of the hit while guiding the clubface squarely into the ball by the proper positioning of the fingers. By allowing the clubhead to lag behind the hands as shown in *Figure C*, all the clubhead speed needed for the distance desired is supplied without strain. This is one of golf's most rewarding shots, the middle iron correctly hit to a green some 160 yards away. It makes for a pleasant walk.

D

This is the vital area where you must know your own abilities with the short irons. While the distance you get with each could possibly overlap, it is always best to let the club do the full job, so that the swing that you so patiently grooved can remain in the correct slot. Otherwise, I feel better using my wedge for the short—and sure—approach.

The Wedge Does All—Almost   The wedge is an American invention and is said to be responsible for being the big reason for the lower scores of today as compared to those recorded in the late twenties. I think that better equipment and more thorough knowledge of the mechanics of golf play an important part in the developing of so many good players, but I agree that the wedge is responsible for shaving off a few of the strokes. It is the heaviest of the clubs, weighing some 17 ounces; it is the shortest, measuring around 34⅝ inches, has the most loft, 54 to 58 degrees, and features the thickest flange on the back of the blade. The flange we will discuss in greater detail in the section on sand, but the wedge comes into its proper spotlight from within the 100 yard range to the pin.

However, too often this club is used indiscriminately and therefore unwisely. It has a critical range within which it will perform according to the skills of the person using it; but beyond that point, it will not produce the type of shot hoped for by the golfer. It is really foolish to expect too much out of the wedge. Beyond the 100 yard range, you'll be better off, more times than not, with another club. Otherwise you will not be using the wedge for its intended purpose: to save strokes.

9

The Pitch
and Chip Maneuvers

With the delicate pitch shots from about 30 to 40 yards from the pin, or perhaps the little flip over a trap, both finesse and timing are needed. This is a shot that can only be developed through a lot of practice because it needs time to master—*if* such skills are ever within one's ability to attain. Take time obtaining "feel" that must go into its execution, and time to reach the point where you have confidence in yourself.

Master the Movement For this shot I would suggest you open your stance somewhat, feet fairly close together, knees relaxed and bent in quite a lot. Move your right toe toward the hole a bit and play the ball approximately at the center of your stance. Here, again, much depends on the type of lie as to how you are going to play the shot. If it is neither good nor bad, use very little hip and shoulder movement: there's no pivot, no conscious effort made to turn away from the ball. Your concern for balance might be minimized, just keep it more toward the heels than toward the toes, a movement which encourages the blade to also move outside the proper line, upsetting your accuracy, but do make a maximum effort to keep your tempo even. Then it is just a matter of taking the club back, breaking the wrists fairly sharply immediately in the backswing (but without any further wrist movement) and from there it is just mainly an arm and hand movement.

Hit Through the Ball   The clubhead is taken back normally, slowly, but returns to contact the ball quite sharply, continuing through and finishing with a partial follow through. There is no need to think about finishing high here. An exception is the shot out of a grassy lie, or from lush clover, or if you are in long rough. These situations call for your hitting through the ball and taking the clubhead on up a little more, making certain that you first get the club going through the grass! It is when the lie is a bit bare that you have to hit down on the ball with very little follow through. If nothing is in your line but fairway and little or no rise, use a less lofted club to chip and run.

Whatever amount of practice time you can spare to learn this shot will reward you in more pars and birdies. Confidence and ability in this shot means you can recover despite missing the green with your approach. A pitch to within two or three feet from the pin will save many shots, needless to say, and this is not too much to strive for. In time you'll find accuracy is more to be expected, and that you will find it pleasurable to pitch those short shots directly at the target. Soon your main concern will be to produce enough elevation to keep the ball moving actively, over any possible trouble areas, and to drop it down on a pre-determined spot on the green so it will then stop somewhere near the hole. This is self-discipline and satisfaction at its best.

The Pitch Shot

Who hasn't hit his drive "so far" or has missed the green "so close" that he has a little "flip shot" left only to miss this delicate approach because that's precisely what he tried to: *"flip it"*? This problem situation calls for rigid—not floppy—wrists: it cannot be "flipped." Firm up, do not loosen up. To get the ball to go up, you have to hit down on it sharply. Develop the feel for this shot through repeated attempts, preferably in practice sessions, and you will have under control golf's most valuable stroke-saving maneuver.

To set up the one-putt salvage, I suggest you open your stance, feet fairly close together, knees relaxed and bent in quite a bit, head over the ball, weight toward the heels. Move your right toe toward the hole somewhat and play the ball approximately in the center of your stance. Much depends on the lie, of course, but, if neither good nor bad, use very little hip and shoulder movement: Make no conscious effort to turn too much away from the ball. Let a relaxation of the knees control this action, but do not stiffen your body so that your hands are under strain in taking the club back and returning it to the ball.

Rhythm is important, so make a maximum effort to keep your tempo even. Starting back, you *do* break the wrists immediately, and fairly sharply, but this is the beginning and the end of such a move. From this point the wrists remain rigidly set until the club has travelled into and through the ball. This delicate shot calls for a firm stroke, and this is best accomplished by creating a large arc with the clubhead. Without breaking the elbows, take the hands back about hip level slowly, then return to the ball with little body movement and contact the ball quite sharply, continuing through and finishing with a partial follow through. There is no need to think about finishing high; yet any jabbing motion with the club will ruin your attempt. Keep your hands moving, your head behind the ball, and let the club's loft do the required lifting. You'll soon be able to drop the ball on a pre-determined spot on the green so it will stop somewhere near the hole.

Chip Shot

The chip shot from the fringe of the green, simple as it seems, has been known to "handcuff" players who, in concentrating so intently on trying to *wish* the ball into the hole, actually suffer from the embarrassing malady known as "mental blackout." This paralysis causes this shot to be stubbed and a stroke to be wasted.

Keep this shot simple. Whenever possible, use a putter. You'll know when it is feasible to do so: when there isn't too much apron between the ball and the green, when the grass is not too high, when the grain is not against you, and when the lie is good. Otherwise, you'll undoubtedly select between a lofted club, like a nine or wedge, or a club with a straighter face, such as a five or six iron. With the former, pick a spot or draw an imaginary circle of any diameter about two-thirds of the way to the pin, stroke the ball to this spot and figure on the ball rolling the remaining one-third distance. With the five or six iron, plan on the ball's landing on a target about one-third of the way to the cup and rolling the remaining two-thirds.

It is too difficult to specify the times when the putter should be used, because it will actually differ with individuals. Some like to stroke the ball going uphill, and fear using the putter when going down green. I would be inclined to reverse the preference, because, when you are looking at a downhill situation, you must consider the fact that the ground behind the ball is higher than the ball itself. With any lofted club, you have to guard yourself against making contact with the ground instead of the ball.

When I can't use the putter, I always go with the wedge, because I find it easier to practice with just one club than with a lot of them. In this way I learn how it will react, I can quickly acquire the "feel" for the shot and can approach this testy situation the same way each time. Distance is easier to judge, also. But whichever club you prefer, follow a plan and then do not compromise with this system. Soon, you'll have the shot under control and, like a lengthy putt, you can expect to make a few now and then.

The Chip Shot Formula   From the apron of the green, I will go with the wedge. If I can't do the job with a putter, that is. The wedge is my choice because I find it easier to practice with one club rather than with a lot of them. I learn how it will react, I can quickly acquire the "feel" for the shot, I can always approach this real tester the same way each time, and I can judge distances more accurately. But this is a matter of personal preference: For the weekend golfer, I do recommend the rolling type clip shot, using a six or seven-iron. But in any case and whenever possible, chip to land the ball on the green, which offers truer bounce, and allow for quite a bit of roll. If you are using the six, you should hit the ball through the air about one-third of the distance and its momentum will move it the remaining two-thirds. With the wedge as I play it, the reverse is true: I hit the ball two-thirds of the way through the air and get one-third roll.

When to Use the Putter These "rules" are standard, not only to goad you into proper club selection, but also to guide you into executing the shot with a plan. This would mean, then, that if you have too much fairway or apron to contend with, the six iron is *not* the club to use. But if it is closer, it doesn't naturally stand that the six iron *is* the proper weapon. Try the putter. As often as I've seen amateurs using a wedge to pitch with when a six-iron would have been better, I believe I've noticed more using a chipping club when they could have successfully used the putter.

The rules for putting when on the apron of the green are common sense ones: Do not use this nearly-straight bladed club when the grain is against you, or when the grass is too high, or when the green is too slick, or when you have too much apron to traverse otherwise, employ the usual putting procedures.

The Tough Grass-Bunker Shot The most difficult of the pitch shots is that one which has the ball nestled in heavy grass not more than a few feet from the putting surface. This shot would be more difficult only if the grass were hairy, with the grain against you and your ball plugged in deep. My choice from this situation is the trusty wedge, hitting into the ball not unlike the method used in a sand trap. Although it might be odd to see someone taking a full cut at such a short shot, it is about the only way to extricate this ball. I hit in behind the ball, keeping the clubhead moving, letting the flange at the bottom of the club cut through the grass and getting the club under the ball which pops up and out. The blade is closed a trifle to prevent the flange from making the club bounce off the grass into the belly of the ball. This is not just a hit and stop shot. A full swing and a follow through is essential.

10
The Hazards of Sand

Just as certain geographical areas boast special varieties of trees, vegetation and weather, they also can be known for certain kinds of sand used in their bunkers. In my travels from New Zealand, first as an amateur in 1958 and 1959 and then as a professional after October, 1960, I have been in and out of light, almost white sand, heavy seaside sand, glassy coral sand, large granuled sand, reddish sand, blackish sand and even sandy sand. Some so fine that even a softly hit ball would almost disappear from view; others so hard you would be afraid the shock of the club hitting into it would break your wrists, but none, of course, that would ever take the place of lush, even fairway.

A Miss Is a Hit Yet, despite these variances, all can be handled in the same tested and proved manner, by executing the shot that calls for *not* contacting the ball. But as simple as this sounds, and despite the fact that some professionals occasionally prefer the sand to an extremely long putt, I admit that this particular shot represents the weakest part of my game. (Do you think I could get away with a claim of heredity? I never had any instruction in my early days. Both my parents were and still are very good golfers, and it was my father who encouraged me and showed me the fundamentals of the game. He now is a five handicap, was as low as two just a few years ago. My mother is now on an eight handicap, which is the lowest she's ever been. She hits a long ball, as far as anybody I've seen, and has a powerful game. She knows all the moves and has all the shots *except for bunker play, which is her big weakness, too.* She has particular trouble when faced with a trap shot out of a bunker with a high lip. She seems unable to get under the ball, to continue her swing so that the ball will rise quickly and drop down on the green. More often than not, she would hit it straight into the face of the trap! Now, since I owe my interest and most of what proficiency I possess to my parents, do you think it might just be possible I owe my sand trap weakness to her?)

The truth of the matter is that in practicing this shot together, we both improved, and of the nine times I was bunkered while playing the British Open, I fortunately came out close enough for one-putt on the first three attempts! Each was most welcome.

The usual sand shot should be played off the right foot from a very open stance, with the clubface open, as well. Take the club straight back from the ball, with a three-quarter swing, and hit the sand approximately an inch and a half behind the ball, with a full swing, continuing without interruption into a very full follow-through. It is important to concentrate on the spot behind the ball, keep the swing smooth and rhythmical *and do not quit.* The trap shot, more than any other, unless it is a curling five foot putt that means the big championship, seems to instill in many golfers a fear that freezes movement, upsets rhythm and balance and blocks out proper thought processes. To them it means they have failed to execute their approach shot properly, and they feel they do not deserve to encounter this extra, uncalled for trouble. Then they accept this punishment, half-heartedly make an attempt to get close to the pin, being content if they merely get out, and continue with their diagnosis of what caused them to veer so much off line. This attitude is dangerous and spirit-shrinking. The sand traps, usually located adjacent to the green, protecting the pin, are often so constructed that they protect the golfer, as well. How often you find them actually sparing your errant golf ball from a much worse fate, like rolling out of bounds, or into some wooded area, or heavy, uncertain rough! While a fairway would be preferred, of course, and occasionally even the rough or hard pan might be easier to contend

Sand Trap

Study the attempts to get out of sand made by members of your Club and you'll probably see two of golf's honored "precepts" proved to complete satisfaction. These "truisms" are: You should not quit on any golf shot, and you usually hit that which you are looking at. Sand traps are credited with causing more anguish than they have reason to. I believe most of this negative-type attitude stems from having seen your approach shot miss the target and fall into the sand, and it is a disappointed person who then faces a situation that at best is sombering. The shot from the sand has to be part of your arsenal, like the art of scrambling, if you ever hope to find the enjoyment of lower scores. First, then, prepare yourself for a full swing, one that picks up speed as the clubhead nears the bottom of the arc. To do so any sooner is like swinging from the top with your longer clubs and the shot will be doomed to failure.

With your body thus ready to handle the weight shift, take care of the second step: Select a target about 1 to 2 inches behind the ball and, without so much as a glance at the ball, hit through that spot. The requirements of this shot are simple: Play the ball off the right foot from an open stance, with the clubface open, as well, and use a sand wedge. Take the club straight back from the ball, or slightly outside, with a three-quarter swing, and hit the *sand* approximately an inch and a half behind the ball, with a full outside-in swing. Continue through without any interruption, looking up only when forced to by the natural flow of the swing. Do not let your attention veer off the spot behind the ball, or let your body sway forward. In either case, the clubhead most likely will make direct contact on the ball. The results will not be to your liking. The sand wedge is the proper tool for this job. It has a wide flange specially designed to let the club ride through the sand and the head is heavy.

You can vary the loft of the "out" as well as the distance the ball will travel by proportionately closing both your stance and the clubface, as you would want to do if the ball is partially buried. You will do well to also play the ball back toward the center of your stance. Make certain you dig in very firmly so that there is no chance of your feet slipping. This will also give you an idea of the texture of the sand, since it is a violation of the Rules of Play to ground your club into the sand prior to the hit. If the sand is extremely loose, however, and your feet dig in deeply, remember to shorten up on your grip, as well.

Do not let yourself have any doubts about whether you will get the ball out of sand, and soon you won't be satisfied with merely getting out, but will begin gearing yourself to pitch up close for a one-putt. Since the texture of sand can vary from one course to another, or even on the same course, learn to identify the differences by inspecting them as often as you can. You can actually feel texture through your feet. You can get to know the feel of the sand wedge riding through the sand by practicing even without a ball. In time you can lessen, if not completely eliminate, the fear of traps by devoting some practice to this shot.

with than some of the lies one could get in sand, no one would choose a penalty stroke to a chance at exploding out of a trap.

The Tailor-Made Sand Wedge I recommend you use a sand wedge for this shot. This is the special, unique club tailor-made to solve most of the sand trap problems. The wide flange is specially designed to let the club ride through the sand; the thick sole prevents the club from becoming embedded, and its invention in the 1930's has helped to lower golf scores. I consider it a definite asset, because it is the proper tool for the job. This means that the odds are decidedly in your favor to get the ball out of the hazard and relatively close to the pin. This begets confidence, the best characteristic a sand trap player can have. I know from experience that if you walk into the bunker with the thought of just getting out, the chances are you'll do just that, and only that. If you are having the trouble my mother was having, this may prove to be an accomplishment; but it won't lead to those par rounds that mean the championships. Since I have adopted positive thinking, things have changed for me, and I feel that when in a trap I've got a good chance of getting close to the pin, that I'm going to get out and down in one putt every time I walk into—and quickly out of—the trap.

Producing the High Loft The next prerequisite is practice, especially for those of us who play different courses in different sections of the world, and for those of you who would be better off learning how to cope with the various and interesting situations that different areas within the bunker can serve up. For the shot that requires high loft and enough distance to travel from 10 to 30 feet, play the ball off the front of your stance, with your feet fairly close together, not more than 18 inches apart. Make certain you dig in very firmly, because your stance must be secure if accuracy is to result. The move away from the ball does not need a very big hip turn; it is mainly a shoulder and arm movement. The tempo should be relatively slow and evenly paced going back, and smooth and firm going into the ball. Remember your target area about one and a half inches behind the ball.

Square Away for Distance When more distance is necessary, move your body more to the left, toward the target, or, in other words, square your stance and also square the clubface. This change in address position also changes the plane of the swing, and the straight-away backswing and downswing takes away the cutting action, resulting in a fairly high lofted shot that will roll. It is about the only safe way to hit from a place in a trap quite removed from the pin that may be tucked up in the far corner, or on the top half of a large two-level, undulating, uphill green.

The Buried Lie This shot is similar to the buried-lie or plugged ball shot, except that less force is needed in its execution. But when the ball plops into heavy sand, making for itself a hole just slightly larger than the ball itself, it is another matter. First, erase all traces of panic, gloom and uncertainty. This ball can be popped out and with less brute strength than is ordinarily imagined. Play the ball in the center or right center of your stance, with the blade hooded (or closed). This will move the flange, created to bounce off the sand in a normal trap shot, farther behind the club's leading edge, thus allowing the wedge to continue through with the flange out of the way, the leading edge of the club will enter the sand first. The sand, which appears to have a solid hold on the ball, can be put to use. When the clubhead makes contact with it about 1″ behind the ball, it creates a sort of "wall" that forces the ball out and up. Do not stop swinging; take the club through without interruption, firmly gripped, and the ball will "pop" out. However, it will come out rather low and with roll. Allow for this, because there is little that can be done to offset it, unless it is to play a bit to the left of the cup and let its hook spin take it in toward the hole. You know, I'm sure, that the 1964 rules endorsed by the United States Golf Association require you remove the pin when hitting from anywhere within 20 yards of the pin as well as from any spot on the green, regardless of distance. This means that you cannot hope to use it as a backboard with a trapshot that is hard to check, such as the one from a buried lie.

11

Don't Underestimate
the Putter

The putter is golf's real stroke saver. To me, it is a veritable life saver. It won for me the playoff for the British Open championship. I played the two extra rounds in 69-71 for a total of 140 to Phil Rodger's 72-74-148, a difference of eight strokes. On the greens I took a total of 57 strokes to Phil's 65, precisely the margin of the victory. I one-putted early in the match, from 6 feet for a par on number one hole, 30 feet for a par on the third, 4 feet for a birdie on four, 8 feet for another birdie on seven and 1 foot for a par on eight. All in all I one-putted on 17 holes, Phil one-putted 8 times; I two-putted 17 times to his 27 two-putt greens and three-putted twice, Phil once.

But if you play golf, I'm sure you know that on each hole you are allowed two strokes with your putter, and that "par" is then figured on the number of shots it takes an average player to reach the green. Thus we have the par threes, short enough to be negotiated in one shot, the par fours, with two shots necessary to get "home," and the par fives, those of such length that ordinarily three strokes are necessary. Then, if the course consists of two par threes, two par fives and the remaining five holes are par fours on each nine, the par for the 18 holes is 72, and half that number are set aside for use by the putter, the shortest but most valuable club in your bag. It is the only club that can be used with equal skill by the small, tall, short, large, professional, amateur, male or female. It is even called the "equalizer," as it is.

Stroke the Ball   All that is required to make a person a good putter is a style that ensures his hitting the ball on the same spot on his putter every time. This would be the beginning. Knowing how to stroke the putt, he then needs only to acquire a knowledge of how to read the green and to judge distance. All this, *and* confidence in himself. A person who knows he's a good putter, usually is. I mean I've *never* seen a good putter who did not think he was good.

All putters, that is the club, itself, whether heavy or light, blade or mallet, steel, hickory or glass shaft, have a spot which gives the most solid hit, and the most solid feel, and the least turn of the face. When the ball is contacted on this spot, it'll roll true. Find this spot, develop your stroke so that you can strike the ball on that particular spot everytime, and you will have solved a major problem.

Two Putting Styles   We normally see two different ways to putt, the arm and shoulder method and the wrist method, and each has its good points and its own list of disciples. I belong to the arms and shoulders group, because I have found it to be consistent for me and completely reliable under the pressures and tensions of tournament golf. Since the putting stroke is quite like a pendulum movement in that the club is taken back straight and returned to the ball straight, entirely with the arms and shoulders, I have no wrist action in the putting stroke at all. But before I continue with my stroke and why I like it, I must stress the fact that there is no set rule one can apply to putting other than sink all attempts! And if you can do that, the whole world will be looking you up. What is done on the putting surface is done according to individual preference, there is no theory that will work for everyone, and what is all right for me may be completely wrong for you. It is such a confined stroke that it can even be practiced indoors, on your living room rug, making it relatively simple for anyone to adopt one style, or at least, try them all, even if he reverts to the one with which he began the sessions.

Putting—B

By squaring everything to the line, feet, hips, shoulders and, of course, putting blade, all you have to do is stroke the ball with enough force to roll the ball to the hole and you won't ever miss. This is theory. Among the factors that might keep the ball from going in are grip, grain and body movement. My grip is the reverse-overlap, as shown, because with it both hands work in unison with each other, and controlling the line is assured. The pressure of the hands on the grip should be firm without any tightness and must be shared equally by both. Being out of balance at this end of the putter causes the other end to mis-direct the ball everytime, and even the fact that the cup is more than twice the diameter of the ball won't always hide this fault. Next of concern is the grain. Experience will teach you best how to "read the green," but the direction the grass is growing will influence the ball, especially as it slows down near the hole. When the grain is against you, the grass will take on a darker appearance, and the putt will require more of a stroke than if you were going *with* the grain. The grass takes on a "light" appearance when the grain is with you. Normally, the grain will run away from mountains, and toward the water. But the biggest and most glaring mistake made by putters the world over is body movement. Sometimes it is easily noticed, as the turning of the shoulders or the shifting of weight, but mostly it is hardly discernible, like that little relaxation of the head, and the fault stays with you to plague you hole after hole.

Learn to take the clubhead back low—raising it too high and too quickly not only gets the ball to spin and swerve, but it also forces incorrect body movement, and the ball has no chance of staying on line,—make contact on the "sweet spot" of the blade and keep your body as still as possible. I vote for the "dying putt" even when in the near vicinity of the hole, but this is a personal choice. I play the ball up forward, and my head stays directly over it. My knees are flexed noticeably, my elbows are kept away from my body, and, although the body does not move before impact, the shoulders and arms do, and once the ball is on its way, I feel an almost imperceptible but rhythmic movement in my legs. However, I am anchored solidly and the putter blade is kept square to the hole. I use and advocate a center-shafted putter.

Just as the stroke, the selection of a putter and the style will vary with different golfers, so will the stance. In fact, I believe it is the least important. However, I like to suggest a square stance with the feet, hips, shoulders, everything square to the line. The reason? Putting can be worked (note I didn't say "solved") on squares: The objective is to select a "line" and hit the ball on this line until it goes into the hole. With a square stance, it'll be easier to place up the blade at right angles to the line and to hit the ball squarely into the hole.

My Tapping Motion I have a fairly long backswing and not too long a follow through, giving me a tapping motion. But there are those who give the ball a short backswing and a long follow through, just the reverse. And, too, there are those who combine the wrist and the shoulder method of putting.

The length of the backswing, naturally enough, depends a lot on how far you are from the hole. The shorter the putt, the shorter the backswing, and the more distance you have to cover, the longer will be the backswing. The pendulum stroking action with a long follow through applies more topspin to the ball than does a long backswing with the short follow through, or tap. And I think that a putt with a lot of overspin is a good method. But I don't worry at all about whether I've got a lot or just a little overspin. It's more a matter of adopting a method for oneself. I just want to stroke the ball into the hole.

How to Read Greens Knowing how to read greens is the real stroke saver, though, and learning all you can about this art can mean the difference between winning big and not making it at all. Travelling throughout the world learning about different types of greens during various seasons has helped me immeasurably; in fact, I consider it the main reason for my being able to putt as I do. But should there be any lack of similar advantages, don't worry. Regardless of grass strain, whether it be bluegrass, Bermuda, Rye, bent or any of the new combinations, a golfer can quickly adjust, provided he can determine the direction of the grain, notice and allow for any "break" or "borrow" between ball and cup, and determine whether the surface putts fast or slow.

In reading greens, remember that the grass, particularly the Bermuda and coarser strains, will grow in a certain direction; normally, it is towards the sun, away from mountains and toward the sea. A note of caution: It is not a good rule of thumb to follow faithfully, yet it is worth thinking about. It should make you aware of some of the hidden tricks a strange course may throw at you if you are totally unwary, which, truthfully, is akin to being careless.

The best way to figure which direction the grass is growing is to read it by the shine. That is, if it is white, you are looking with the grain, and if it is very dark, a deep shade of green, you

Putting—A

The golfer spends more time lining up his putt than he does for any other shot. This is true even if he is of the "miss 'em quick" school. With this much time on his hands, or mind, he has to be careful that his thoughts are concerned merely with the only two considerations of the problem: line and distance, and, of these, the question of distance is the one that must be answered more often than not, surprising as this may sound.

Once I have determined this to the best of my ability, I then don't waste too much time or thought in the execution of that shot. I stroke the club through the ball with the momentum and line I had visualized, and when carried out as planned, I fully expect to hole the putt. This attitude is necessary if a golfer is ever going to succeed as a putter. I'm sure I don't have to tell you that the putts you think you are going to miss usually do not find the hole. Putting is an individualistic art: what is correct for me might be completely wrong for you. Of the two methods: the "wrist," and the arms and shoulder, I belong to the latter because I have found it to be consistent and reliable for me under the pressures of tournament golf. But ask the wrist players why they prefer and use that system, and they will undoubtedly say the same thing! I use a fairly long backswing and ordinarily limit the length of the follow through, giving me, in effect, a tapping motion. Upon making contact with the ball, I have reached the end of being able to exert any influence over its line and speed, and this gives the impression that my head comes up off the ball too quickly. This is not the case at all. Keeping the head absolutely still during the course of the putting stroke is mandatory. You do not stand a chance if you allow it to move even the slightest. I want to make this point clear, because it is probably the only thing in the entire putting stroke that consistent golfers have in common: Very few have the same grip, stance, address, method of stroking the ball, even models of putter; but everyone does all he can to "lock" himself into an unmoveable position so the blade can remain on line going back, returning to the ball, and into the follow-through. For this reason, and regardless of your choice of putters or of stroke, I suggest the square stance with the feet, hips, shoulders, all square to the line. (Figure "B") In this manner, you can more easily place the blade of the club at right angles to this line and hit the ball squarely into the hole.

are going into or against the grain. When extreme doubt exists, check the hole, itself. You can easily notice the way the grain is growing. In fact, this is what the touring professional is checking when he is seen peering intently into the $4\frac{1}{4}$ inch cavity into which he is trying to "lose" his ball.

Another factor that influences the roll of the ball is the manner in which some courses cut their greens. For instance, at the Augusta National course in Georgia, the site of the famed Masters tournament, the greens are cut up and down and also crossways. This makes it extremely difficult to detect any grain, or its direction. Now, it may be an asset in that it can eliminate the necessity to concern yourself about it except in the immediate vicinity of the hole, and you can spot the direction by looking into the cup and checking the grain above the dirt line. On greens that are cut in two directions only, a definite knap is produced that is much easier to detect, and one has merely to allow for it as he putts.

Beware the Slow-Down Area   Going with the grain, the putt will be stroked much easier than when you have to hit into it, and should you be putting across grain, make the allowance depending on the length of the putt and the strength of the grain. Be mindful of the fact that the grain will have little effect on the ball as it leaves the putter blade when it is travelling at maximum speed, but, when it begins to slow down, the green pulls it in the direction of the grain and a putt that is timidly hit may twist crazily at the hole. This is why some putts of rather short length fail to drop.

As stated previously the length of the backswing will depend in good measure on how far you are from the hole. The shorter the putt, of course, the shorter the backswing. But on the short ones on Bermuda green, you must always be firm; you must always putt the ball to go into the hole. On ordinary putts, however, I prefer to lag the ball. I feel that a dying putt has much more chance of dropping in the hole than does a putt which is running fast for the hole and just catches the lip. In this case, the dying putt will go in every time, whereas the other will hit the rim and spin around and stay up, sometimes not even close enough for comfort. I hit them in much more softly than most other tournament golfers do, even the short ones, unless on coarse Bermuda grass that is grainy, I just like to trickle in the hole. I definitely am not a charge putter, but, here too, it is a matter of individual taste, and I won't insist that my way is right. But I will say that the weekend golfer whose skills might be rusted by inactivity could employ the lag putting technique to better advantage than he would charging the ball, and to leave the charging putt for the person who feels he can always hole the one coming back. If you are confident in your putting, bang it under the "never up, never in" philosophy. If not, lag it up and let it die in the hole.

My Style and Putter Preference As with all my other shots, I play the ball up forward, in front of my right foot, and my head stays directly over the ball. The type of putter that fits best with my style is a center shafted blade that, perhaps surprisingly, does not have an upright lie. My knees are flexed noticeably, my elbows are kept close to my body, and, although the body does not move before impact, the shoulders and arms do. I am solidly anchored, however, and the putter blade is always, when I'm putting well, that is, kept square to the line, both going back and returning into and through the ball. I have been successful using this putting style and this style of putter, and I'll keep on doing both even though some days I'm better than others, even though other members of my group might hole out more putts than I with a style or a putter that is quite different, and even though the greens change noticeably. Some of my friends switch to a blade from a mallet when they move from heavy, slow greens to those that are fast, but I haven't, and do not intend to. I sincerely advocate the center shafted putter because with this style it is easier to strike the ball solidly every time; the sweet spot is at the end of the shaft in the center of the club, and hitting the ball with the sweet spot is, as much as anything else, the secret to consistent putting.

12

You Against the Course

Golf course architecture is truly amazing, especially on the courses throughout the world considered to be "championship" in every detail. Without mentioning them by name, those with true character will feature holes of different lengths to force the use of practically every club in the bag, with rewards awaiting those who can maneuver the ball and who are willing to gamble, doglegs that can save as much as 40 yards on the well-placed tee shots, fairway bunkers that will catch an errant drive but which will, nonetheless, open toward the end nearest the green to give the player a possible chance to make up for his driving error, albeit it by executing one of golf's most difficult shots, a wood or long iron from sand.

The "big" courses might also feature greens that are large when the fairway is the toughest, small, undulating putting surfaces when it is fairly easy to get to, and trapped not only to demand the most accurate shot from the player, but, in many cases, to protect him from a fate much worse than blasting from a bunker: In the event you haven't always noticed, at times a stretch of sand that magnetizes your ball is the only decent area between your ball and water, or woods, or rough, or out of bounds.

But it is often those "hidden" places that can mean the difference between your putting for a birdie or a bogey. I mean the little hills or mounds or valleys that are out there where they can influence the roll or lack of roll of your tee shot. How often it happens. Had your tee shot landed a few yards farther or stopped shorter, it would have rolled to a level spot, instead of leaving you with a downhill lie, or a longer shot to the green, or both. Then, too, there are those situations whereby the only level shot to the pin is offered by the side of the fairway farthest from the green, posing another type of problem that must be resolved.

Study the Battleground   If it isn't within your skills to place the golf ball where you want to, and this just about includes all of us, the least you can do is to make yourself aware that these areas exist. The method is to pace off each fairway, somewhat in the manner the touring professionals do. Because we play a different course every week, we can't adjust to distances as readily as those of you who play the same course week in and week out. Guesswork doesn't belong in our way of life, therefore, to eliminate as much uncertainty as we can, we pace off the distances for ourselves. As you know, we cannot consult anyone but our caddie regarding distances. It isn't like those other times when we could ask our partner what club he thought should be selected. But then, perhaps it is just as well.

An Exposé of Two Scoundrels   I remember hearing of two situations that make me wonder if anyone can be trusted to give the correct answer. I've been told the story about one golfer who got so tired of constantly being asked what club he used on his shots that he ordered a set of irons all marked with the same number-*eight!* He therefore had one answer to every question, regardless of how far or in what trajectory the ball travelled. Another clever golfer, perhaps to deliberately confuse his opponent but more likely to hide the fact he was not hitting as far as he used to hit, ordered a set of irons that featured a straighter loft than the particular number called for. Thus, his two-iron had the face loft of a one, his three-iron the loft of a normal two-iron, etc. You can imagine what went through the minds of those with whom he was playing, as he nonchalantly stroked a nine-iron to the stick. And confusion causes as many bad shots as faulty footwork.

Check the Scorecard Plotting a course begins before you leave the clubhouse, by scanning the scorecard and noting the lengths of the holes, the over-all length of the course, and the "stroke" or "handicap" number assigned to each hole. Thus the hole which is the hardest on the course will be given handicap number 1, the easiest number 18. If you are giving strokes to or getting strokes from your playing partner, you should award or receive them according to where they fall on the card. You'll notice that one nine will show only even numbers, the other odd numbers, so that if there is a two stroke difference between two men, the one with the higher handicap will be given one stroke on each nine.

Playing Cards

Better golf may be in the cards for you. A check of the scorecard before you play is almost as important to the club member or fees paying customer as pacing off the course is to us touring professionals. Obviously, it won't disclose the location of dog-legs, water, bunkers, trees, undulations and other problems, but it does show yardage and how each hole is rated as to toughness.

Hole	Yardage	Bogey	Par	Handcp Strokes	Self	Partner	Opp A	Opp B
1	390	5	4	7				
2	157	4	3	15				
3	452	5	5	3				
4	346	5	4	9				
5	130	3	3	17				
6	362	5	4	5				
7	318	5	4	13				
8	343	5	4	11				
9	377	5	4	1				
Out	2875	42	35					
10	163	4	3	18				
11	419	5	4	2				
12	412	5	4	6				
13	315	5	4	12				
14	200	4	3	10				
15	185	4	3	16				
16	295	5	4	14				
17	449	5	5	4				
18	375	5	4	8				
In	2813	42	34					
Out	2875	42	35					
Total	5688	84	69					

PLEASE REPLACE TURF AND SMOOTH OUT SAND IN TRAPS

HANDICAP

NET SCORE

A

ARONIMINK Newtown Square Penna. MEN	HOLE	SELF	PART	±	STROKES	±	OPP	OPP	PAR	DISTANCE LONG	REGULAR	SHORT
APACHE	1				3				4	432	412	400
PUEBLO	2				15				4	383	363	348
NAVAJO	3				5				4	442	422	396
SEMINOLE	4				1				4	457	410	398
MOHAWK	5				17				3	162	145	135
COMANCHE	6				11				4	396	381	368
SHAWNEE	7				13				4	370	360	350
SITTING BULL	8				7				3	233	215	200
KICKAPOO	9				9				5	610	515	442
	Out								35	3485	3223	3037
CHEROKEE	10				6				4	449	419	409
KIOWEA	11				8				4	411	380	370
SAGINAW	12				4				4	459	423	409
BLACKFOOT	13				12				4	384	370	337
IROQUOIS	14				16				3	211	195	184
LENAPE	15				2				4	469	428	390
SIOUX	16				10				5	541	514	496
SENECA	17				18				3	213	175	156
ARONIMINK	18				14				4	423	396	380
	In								35	3560	3300	3131
TOTAL									70	7045	6523	6168
HANDICAP				DATE								
NET												

				SCORES								
PLAYERS MUST KEEP ELECTRIC CARTS AT LEAST 25 FEET FROM GREENS.				SELF	PART.	SIDE MATCHES WE / THEY		OPP'T	OPP'T	PLAYERS MUST KEEP ELECTRIC CARTS OFF TEES.		
MEN										WOMEN		
HDCP.	REGULAR TEES	BACK TEES	PAR			HOLE				PAR	YARDS	HDCP.
11	336	343	4			1				4	246	11
1	591	594	5			2				5	528	1
17	125	130	3			3				3	118	17
3	384	390	4			4				4	378	3
5	396	402	4			5				4	390	5
9	361	367	4			6				4	355	9
13	506	523	5			7				5	482	13
7	422	435	4			8				4	390	7
15	148	155	3			9				3	142	15
	3269	3339	36			OUT				36	3029	
10	412	425	4			10				4	382	10
12	340	345	4			11				4	340	12
4	410	421	4			12				5	390	4
16	217	225	3			13				3	187	16
18	315	320	4			14				4	311	18
6	405	413	4			15				4	379	6
2	425	433	4			16				5	399	2
8	490	498	5			17				5	378	8
14	193	199	3			18				3	130	14
	3207	3279	35			IN				37	2897	
	6476	6618	71			TOT.				73	5926	

PLAYERS MUST:
1. Let faster players through.
2. Smooth traps.
3. Repair ball marks on greens.

HANDICAP

NET SCORE

Player_____ Attested_____ Date _____

HOLE	BLUE COURSE	WHITE COURSE	PAR	STROKES						Won + Lost −
1	455	449	5	15						
2	442	416	4	5						
3	569	532	5	3						
4	141	135	3	17						
5	328	319	4	11						
6	431	402	4	7						
7	180	162	3	13						
8	454	429	4	1						
9	414	385	4	9						
OUT	3414	3229	36							

Smooth Out All Footprints Made in Traps

HOLE	BLUE COURSE	WHITE COURSE	PAR	STROKES						
10	491	476	5	10						
11	392	357	4	16						
12	436	382	4	2						
13	211	190	3	6						
14	362	347	4	12						
15	392	380	4	14						
16	129	118	3	18						
17	430	408	4	4						
18	391	375	4	8						
IN	3234	3033	35							
OUT	3414	3229	36							
TOT	6648	6262	71							

PLAYER_____

ATTESTED_____DATE_____

PLEASE REPLACE TURF

LONGSHORE CLUB PARK

MEN'S COURSE				SCORES					LADIES' COURSE		
HCP.	YDS.	PAR	SELF	FART.	±	HOLE	OPP.T	OPP.Y	PAR	YDS.	HCP.
13	266	4				1			4	266	13
15	150	3				2			3	150	15
7	410	4				3			5	401	7
11	280	4				4			4	280	11
9	320	4				5			4	320	9
1	420	4				6			5	420	3
3	530	5				7			5	475	1
17	130	3				8			3	130	17
5	375	4				9			4	375	5
—	2881	35				OUT			37	2817	—
8	470	5				10			5	445	2
14	200	3				11			3	160	14
10	305	4				12			4	240	12
12	201	3				13			3	150	16
2	428	4				14			5	428	4
18	170	3				15			3	142	18
4	420	4				16			4	330	6
6	360	4				17			4	280	10
16	290	4				18			4	290	8
—	2844	34				IN			35	2465	—
—	5725	69				TOTAL			72	5282	—

MCR		HCP		WCR
67		NET		70

Date	Scorer

Attest

Look at the figures in the column marked "Strokes" or "Handicap." The odd-numbered stroke holes appear on the front nine, the even numbered ones on the back, and are usually assigned fairly early as to be of use to the person receiving them. According to the Rules, stroke hole #1 is the hole that has been proved the most difficult to score on and is not necessarily the most difficult to par. Generally, then, the hole rated as "toughest" would be a par-5. When it isn't, as is the case in all but one of the five examples illustrated, you can look forward to a severe test. Whenever it is possible, the lower-numbered strokes appear near the middle or beginning of the two nines.

The most unusual stroke assignment appears on Card B. The longest hole on the course, the ninth, at either 442, 515 or 610 yards depending whether playing the short, regular or long course, is accorded Stroke #9, meaning that it is easier to score on than *four* other holes on the front side despite its length. And a similar oddity occurs on the back nine. The 16th hole, at 496, 514 and 541 yards, respectively, apparently plays easier than four shorter holes on the back nine.

On Card C, the fourth hole will require some further explanation. At 384 yards, it is shorter than four other holes, but has been rated as being the second toughest of the front nine holes to score on.

On cards D and A the Stroke #1 hole has been assigned to the eighth and ninth holes respectively, signifying that their toughness is so established that they deserve this description despite their appearing at the end or so near the end of the front nine, and despite the fact that neither is the longest hole.

The interesting feature of Card E is that its par, based on "round" numbers for each hole, is 69 but its "rating," a total of the description of difficulty of each hole listed in fractions by the association rating the course, is a 67. The next time you play a new course, or even your own, take a long look at the scorecard. You may learn a secret or two that will be as helpful to your score as a few long putts.

Pace Off Distances   It will also help to know how far you hit a tee shot, but if this is hard to determine, you can pace off the remaining distance to the green (or figure it from any known yardage marker), subtract that yardage from the total yardage evidenced on the card and you'll have the length of your drive. However, it is the distance that remains between your ball and your target that is of prime importance to the one interested in selecting the correct club. If you are playing your home course, it should be relatively easy; but if you are on a strange layout, then it will pay to check this out yourself.

Pick up a tree or a fairway trap or any permanent object that is easy to spot and pace off the distance from that place to the middle of the green. Mark this clearly on a card and keep it handy for quick reference. Include notes on locations of fairway hazards, sand traps, length of rough, the best method of approaching, and any other pertinent information, such as potential pin placements, size and undulations of green, direction of grain and direction of prevailing wind. But even all this is not enough. Determine whether the green is one-club or two-club size, that is, is it large enough to be reached with either of two clubs. This knowledge will serve you when the pin is in front or in back, protected by a trap, or on days when the wind is a factor. It will also help avoid the trouble that may be in front, to either side or to the rear.

This is the only way to eliminate guesswork, and I recommend this procedure highly. It stands to reason that if two persons of equal ability were to play a match at the home course of one, the man with "local knowledge" will have the odds in his favor. Learn all you can about your course. Just do not select the busiest day of the year to do your figuring.

All Hits Aren't Perfect   In selecting a club, too many golfers will choose the one that will require their hitting their best shot. Don't. In a round of golf, even the experts hit very few of what can be considered "perfect" shots—the successful ones are only those who have reduced the number of "missed" ones, so, in remembering that your best shot is not going to be produced 90 percent of the times, go with the little longer club. One of golf's biggest stroke savers, really, is to make the shot a little easier by using a club that will ensure your avoiding whatever trouble there is, wherever it is.

Swing Easy—Score Better   It is also important that once you do make a club selection, you are convinced in your own mind that you do have the right club. Indecision can ruin you and your game. If you're tossing up between a four and a five iron, for example, and you are playing into a wind, and the five iron you decide to go with has to be hit perfectly, not only is there a good chance that you will fall short, you might also (or instead) miss the shot. If you are ever undecided under most circumstances, take the longer club and swing easier. You will feel better, stroke the ball better and begin scoring better. It has been proven that more often than not a wrong club selection results in a man being short of the green rather than being too long. Therefore, I suggest, rather, I urge you to use that little longer club, swing a little smoother, and get it up there.

13
Those "Different" Shots

The left-hander usually will not find himself handicapped because of the way he has to stand to the ball. As already mentioned, occasionally a hole will dogleg in the wrong direction for us, and the shot that would put *us* into proper position will be the one shot that does not produce any distance at all. But, otherwise, the golf courses are true tests that continually challenge the player from tee to green, and it will pay him to plan how to attack each hole well in advance.

But even the best laid plans go awry, it's been said, and I think it was so stated with a golfer in mind. Meaning there's more to the golf course than tee, fairway and green, and when you find yourself off the track and in trouble, it calls not only for knowing how to come up with the proper shot, but how to keep your mental processes uncluttered.

My Safe but Sorry Shot Once, I recall, I concentrated on a problem shot too much. In a recent tournament I drove the ball into the rough on the right and, in checking, noticed that my path to the green was blocked somewhat by a tree. It meant I would have to draw (hook) my ball about 20 feet, but that isn't too much. I was figuring on using a 3-iron. Having thus taken care of the "line," I then re-checked the lie to make certain I could maneuver the ball. It is one thing to have an opening,

89

quite another to have the proper lie, and in this case, it wasn't as good as it looked to be at first glance. The ball was nestled on long grass and setting up well, yet I was very hesitant about what might happen when it came out. The few loose strands of grass in sight made me wonder if there were any tree roots under the ball. You must realize this had suddenly come as an additional concern: The tree which was partially blocking my line I had solved immediately; but now, the lie continued to bother me. At the last moment, then, just before hitting the ball, I completely ignored the tree and centered my attention on just getting the ball out. The ball flew out just as I hoped it would, but I had forgotten about my line and sure enough, the ball hit the tree solidly and it ricocheted into even worse trouble.

I don't think there is any situation any more depressing in all of golf than the one whereby you carelessly ignore an obvious problem, unless, perhaps, it is the one which sees you playing it safe only to run into the very problem you are trying to avoid, as witness my hitting the aforementioned three-wood out of bounds during the British Open. Or you might consider, as a foolhardy act, the changing of one's plan. The trouble that I found myself in was on the opposite side of the fairway from the one I had originally intended to favor should my drive go off line in the first place! While the right side of this particular hole gave a more open and shorter shot to the green, some 465 yards from the tee, it meant that all of me would be standing in the rough and against trees during any attempt to get out. So how did I get there?

I hooked my tee shot, I think, because I was trying to bite off a bit too much. I thought a birdie might win the tournament for me. Anyway, I was still in the rough on my third shot and blocked by another tree. But, fortunately, the ball was setting up well enough to allow me to concentrate *only* on hooking it around the obstacle. I used a 4-iron to go the 160 yards and the hook I needed came off very well, the ball stopping on the green and the long approach putt nearly went. I gladly and thankfully took a bogey under the circumstances, and I finished the 72 hole event tied for fifth place, good enough for $2,200 purse. Had I done better by as little as one stroke anywhere during the tournament, an additional $300 or $400 would have been mine. A double bogey, which the two mistakes on that one hole could easily have cost me, would have given me between $300 and $400 less, such is the method of determining prize money.

Making the Ball Bend Once a group of golfers was sitting around a table in the clubhouse and the talk centered around the various ways to deliberately hook and slice. Theory after theory was offered by six or seven of the amateurs. One said he crowded the ball to get it into a roundhouse hook and reached for it to make it fade. Another confided that the best way to "bend it" to the left was to keep the shoulders level and the knees rigid, and to hook he merely would stiffen the wrists and elbows, and a third changed his grip. The debate was going at a fast clip when a member of the party who had silently endured all that was being said, suddenly bolted upright, slammed the palm of his hand loudly on the table top and yelled, "Can't any of you blasted idiots tell me how to hit a straight ball!"

The simple truth among the majority of golfers is that it *is* easier to hook and to slice and too much of a challenge to knock the ball straight. Just stand at almost any tee and watch the foursome drive off. Sometimes not one shot goes straight. But of course it is never done intentionally.

Up to this point we have discussed only positive actions, suggesting only the few things which must be kept in mind to develop a repeating swing that will stand up under the pressure of play. This is also known as "feel," and if the swing goes off slightly, the ball will be so affected. It is around this principle, this truth, that most of the touring professionals have devised their way of maneuvering the ball: Because they come into the ball the same way most every time, they consistently hit the straight ball, and any variation in stance and swing would cause the ball to go off line. This is how the pros do it. To hook the ball, that is, draw it from left to right, close your stance by pulling the left foot back from the line of flight and swing inside-out. Occasionally I might also close the clubface slightly, and will roll my wrists after impact to accentuate the degree of bend I want to put on the ball. If I want to fade, I would take the club absolutely straight from the ball and return it on the outside of the line of flight, concentrating on cutting across the ball without using too much left hand in the shot, all from an open stance.

Don't Tamper with Your Grip   It is not suggested you tamper with your grip by moving the hands into the "weak" position, more to your right and on top of the shaft to help produce a fade, or into the "strong" position by moving both hands more to the left, under the shaft, to obtain a hook.

It perhaps wasn't too easy to find the proper grip. Now that you have it correctly aligned and perfectly attuned to give you maximum consistency, leave it alone. To make the ball move to the right or left, change only your stance and the swing plane. And the next time you get out to the practice area, you can help yourself understand how to hit them straight if you spend more time "deliberately" making the ball bend.

HILLY LIES

Just as the conditions above the ground are always subject to change, so are those *on* the ground. Sometimes the ups and downs of Mother Nature's weather, explained in a later chapter, are easier to contend with than the ups and downs of golf course fairways. I'm referring to those hilly lies that make the game more interesting.

The uphill, sidehill and downhill shots, when they appear with more than usual frequency in a round, can do as much to your score, the wrong way, as wind and rain combined. Most of the world's great courses feature undulating fairways, thus posing this problem for everyone, and so it will always be as long as golf is being played. The golfer who has the know-how to play these shots is going to find himself at home wherever he goes.

Downhill—Level the Hips   The toughest of these situations is the downhill shot, especially if length is also required. Again, my type of upright swing saves the day more so than for the flat swinger who, in dragging the club back low, risks hitting the rising ground behind him. He may try to offset this danger by straightening out his backswing, thus placing him in a different plane and he will either hook or pull or fail to get full blade behind the shot. Most knowing golfers will bend the back knee, the left in my case, to level the line of the hips. Then with the ball played a bit left of center because the club will contact it first, the club is taken back fairly normal, unless the contour rules otherwise. The swing into the ball should be smooth and uninterrupted, with the clubhead following the ground's contour. Move that clubhead through the ball, without lifting or raising the body at impact. The hands generally precede the clubhead. Because of this, the shot should produce roll, and the club selected might be one less than normal. The chief fault, it would be easy to see, is hitting behind the ball. Maintain balance and a steady head position, hit through the ball rhythmically, and another of golf's rewarding shots will be yours.

Uphill, Restrict the Backswing Going uphill requires your playing the ball up forward, unless you already do so, as I. The pull of gravity will force the weight to move back to your left side, so make certain it does not buckle your knee further to the left. Keep the weight on the inside of the left foot and restrict the backswing so that you do not sway going back, and open your stance a little. The backswing is otherwise normal as regards plane, so return to the ball as always, with a slight change in the positions of the hands if you wish to keep the ball low—move them ahead of the blade, or high—keep them slightly behind the blade. The selection of clubs is just the reverse from the downhill lie: The ball will travel in a higher trajectory and not as far, therefore, use a club a little longer than you would normally.

One of the hardest uphill shots is the delicate one with a lofted club, such as a nine-iron or wedge. It is easy to succumb to the impulse to pick the ball up or, worse, to beat down on it. Both of these faults can be checked, possibly eliminated, by an open stance, a balanced restricted backswing, a slight pause at the top, and a right hand lead through the ball with a firm two-handed grip on the club. Turn the shoulders and knees on the backswing to a degree in keeping with your normal turn and with the distance needed. Do not "freeze" on this shot, and do not try to help by a lift with the body or hands the club blade produce the needed loft.

Sidehill Solutions The sidehill lies are perplexing, and the situation with the ball lower than the feet is particularly difficult. The tendency here is to push or slice the ball, since the pull of gravity is to the left of target encouraging the plane of the swing to come from the outside. Allow for this. Move your entire stance to the right as though you were aiming for a spot to the right of the green, get your weight more on the heels and make full contact with the ball. It should drift to the left and if your club selection is good, will take you onto the putting surface.

But when the ball is higher than your toes, the swing flattens, you are forced to stand a little farther from the ball, and a hook is generally the result. Change your stance so that you are aiming to the left of the green, choke up on a longer club, likewise shorten your swing and play the ball a bit left of center.

Rough

If the left-hander's tee shot is destined to go off the fairway, he'd be better off straying to the left. Then, unless his error was very great, he would at least be *standing* in or near the fairway and away from problems as trees and bushes. It is bad enough that the ball be nestled in the rough, without your having to back up against an unyielding object. If the ball *is* in thick grass, discount any idea of going for distance, don't even consider using a wood or long iron; instead, be satisfied with positioning your next shot for a better approach to the green. The problem here is two-fold: You have to take the club into the air rather abruptly on the backswing so as not to snarl in the grass, and you must bring the clubface down sharply on the ball so it will rise quickly without danger of burrowing in deeper. At times when the grass is high but thin and not too resistant, you might get away with using a wood. This club has a long shaft and can build up clubhead speed easily, the head can cut a swath through the grass, and there is enough weight and loft to ride through the grass and get into the ball without strain.

From about 150 yards out, play this shot as much like a fairway shot as you can, with the same body turn, weight shift and follow through. The circumstances of the lie and general conditions of play, as well as what's at stake, must be considered, of course. But the ball normally will not travel as high as the same shot from the fairway, and it will roll much farther. It is difficult to control a shot from the rough, but it is all part of the game, so don't let your spirits lag when the ball bounces into the heavier grass.

Playing a shot from the rough when it's within sixty yards of the green is much more difficult. The distance requires a full shot; but you aren't certain of what lies under the ball, and you can never be sure how the ball or the club will react. It would be rather wise to use a nine-iron rather than the wedge, which, with its heavy flange, might bounce off the ground or off the packed, thick grass and skull the ball. The *sharper* leading edge of the nine-iron is more suited to handle this problem, and the results can be much more consistently judged. If the grass is so thick it hides a good portion of the ball, make sure you correctly identify the ball as yours before you hit. It is legal to do so. Playing the wrong ball can cost you the hole in match play or two strokes in stroke play. And that would be really rough.

ROUGH IS TOUGH

The ball that finds its way into the rough close to the green might be the finish of an extra long tee shot, thereby presenting a chance at a birdie *if* you get out in good shape. Or it might be a wayward approach shot, meaning that you will have to recover handsomely if you are going to save your par. In either case, knowing how to cope with this shot is often the difference between winning and losing, and further emphasis on its importance is not necessary.

Never Give Up   The game of golf is a game where you always have a chance either to win holes or save strokes right to the very end. It is with this mental attitude that I play the game. It helps me accept the bad with the good. I am aware that I'm going to hit a lot of bad shots and that I am going to make a lot of mistakes in a round of golf, but I am also convinced that these same errors can be overcome by making a successful recovery. Try this attitude yourself. If you are six down, try to make it five, and if you are one up, work to make it two.

The Wedge or Nine Iron?   If the rough is too high or too thick, you have no alternative but to play it safe and set yourself up for the next shot. Otherwise, maintain your composure and follow a plan. But along with philosophy, a certain amount of skill is needed, especially when you find yourself off the fairway and in tall grass.

Decide whether you should utilize the cutting action of the nine-iron's leading edge or whether you need the weight of the heavy flanged wedge to slam into the ball. Generally, the nine-iron will produce shots that are more consistent in roll, length and force. When the grass is high, take the clubhead back in a more abrupt arc, returning to the ball sharply to get it airborne quickly. Continue to swing through without interruption, and the ball should have quick loft, coming out of the rough without any additional entanglements. Be careful, however, of your selection of clubs: Remember the nine-iron will cut through the grass, the wedge with its many flanges may bounce off the ground and "skull" the ball.

The weight is either evenly distributed or in toward the heels slightly to offset any body motion toward the ball. A forward tilt of the body pushes the blade outside the line and encourages an occasional hit on the hosel of the club. You all know what this produces—a ball that goes sharply off to the left, almost laterally away from your target. The approach shot from the rough requires a smooth, even tempo and a right hand lead throughout the entire swing. As the saying goes, never let your left hand pass the right as you swing through the ball.

Should the rough be sandy, hitting down sharply on the ball will be futile. Sandy rough has less give than does the normal rough. In this instance, take more club than usual to give you distance with a shorter swing. The ball must be hit squarely when the club is almost at the bottom of the arc, so stay with this shot all the way, keep your balance and, once again, follow through.

14
Those "Different" Days

You already know that I play the ball off my right foot with practically all my clubs, from the driver down through the wedge. This not only enables me to keep the clubhead as precisely in the same plane both ways as is possible, it also produces a high shot, one that goes up into the air where there is less trouble than can be found on the ground. There are no sand traps up there. The ball that travels in a high trajectory might not roll too much after hitting on the fairway, thus sacrificing a little distance, but neither will it continue to move off the fairway or off the green, thus avoiding more trouble than a ball that continues to move. I'm sure everyone has hit a low approach shot that caught the green in fine shape, only to skid through and end up in a trap, or one that hit the face of an incline and kicked back into sand, rough, water or worse. But if you had hit that high ball, one that will come down *on* the green and almost sit where it lands, you will have for yourself a shot that is more easily controlled and one that is more dependable.

WHEN THE WIND BLOWS

There are, of course, occasions when it is necessary to use a low, travelling shot. One, when you have to hit into a wind, and two, when you have to keep it low to avoid some tree branches or other types of problems. When faced with this prospect, I play the ball back toward my left foot only to make certain that I keep my hands moving well in front of the clubhead. Hitting the ball more on the downswing will produce a ball with a much lower trajectory, whether your swing is upright, like mine, or flat.

Generally, in the United States, wind is not such a big problem as it is on the seaside courses of Great Britain where they play the British Open, but wind anywhere in the world will raise havoc with golfers. It has the tendency to do the same thing to golf scores. The only consolation is that it is the same for everyone. So, if you are scoring badly in the wind you must think there are a lot of others who are also playing badly because of the conditions.

Hitting Into the Breeze   The wind that comes directly at you will make the ball do strange things, emphasizing, as it does, any slight mistake you might have made in hitting the ball, turning what could have been a little fade or draw into a roundhouse slice or wicked hook. Into the teeth of a wind, then, widen your stance for better balance, shorten your backswing as an additional aid to balance, keep the weight well on your right side, take at least one club more than you ordinarily would from that same spot, and do not force your swing. Firm everything up, concentrate on a shorter backswing and you'll find that you will pivot less, won't turn away from the ball as much, your footwork will be more secure and you should hit the ball a lot crisper. Oh yes, do not look up too soon: You might not like what you see.

If you are hitting an approach into the green with the wind blowing in at you, hit straight for the pin. With the normal backspin on the ball greatly intensified by the wind, you can be certain the ball is going to hit on, dance and settle down quickly.

The Downwind Floaters   Downwind approach shots can be tougher, less desirable than those hit into the wind. All of the helpful spin put on the ball by the headwind is taken away as the ball is carried aloft. It floats longer but is almost uncontrollable. Allow for a maximum amount of roll. You can further help matters by using a more lofted club than normal, and resist the temptation to rush the shot and come up off the ball. Keep your head down: You can be certain that if the ball is hit properly, you are going to get the needed distance, and if you are on the tee that it'll be easier to do so.

Don't Forget the Crosswinds　The crosswind poses problems that are similar yet uniquely different. This challenge can be blowing directly across from either right to left or left to right, or be part of a downwind or a headwind. Whichever is the case, play *with* it, do not try to hold the ball into it. It would be folly to try to hook a ball into a wind that is blowing from right to left, and vice-versa. Similarly, if it is coming from in front or from behind at an oblique angle, make the necessary compensations, playing it to bring the ball into the target area *according to its own velocity*. Do not fight it.

WHEN THE RAIN DAMPENS

Another bad weather condition is rain, and as it is with wind, its effect on you mentally is as important as the effects physically. No one likes to be subjected to the whims of a rainstorm, or to have to don special rainwear, hold onto an umbrella, cover the head, take along a batch of towels and slosh around 18 holes of wet, miserable golf. But your biggest ally can be your attitude. If this type of weather will dampen your spirits as well as your body, you will be in for a rough time, mentally, physically and statistically. You cannot hope to maintain your concentration and think clearly enough to offset the bad conditions and save strokes through keen judgment unless you make the best of the conditions.

Keep Yourself and Clubs Dry　When playing in rain, keep not only yourself dry but also your clubs, as well. There is plenty of wet weather equipment available to keep everything dry; it weighs only a few ounces and can be rolled into a package small enough to fit in the boot pocket of your bag. Wear rubber golf shoes or rubbers that have spikes or nubs and which can fit over your street shoes. However, if your golf shoes are quality, you will find that they will withstand much of the moisture encountered even on a nasty day. Should the leather shoes get wet, place wood shoe trees inside and let them dry in normal room temperature. This means a golfer should have and use at least two pair of shoes. I say this is a minimum requirement.

Not only must you keep your hands and the grip on your club as dry as possible to preclude the club's slipping out of your grasp, and today's good composition grips go a long way in helping just this sort of situation, but you must also keep the clubface dry, too. When water fills the face scoring, that is, those lines that run across the blade, the ball will fly off without any spin and consequently without any control. It is permissible to wipe the clubface before each shot, and it is recommended you do so. However, the ball will tend to fly because of the moisture it is bound to pick up. Under such a circumstance, allow for some extra run, play the ball for the front of the green rather than for the flag. My method of hitting, with the ball played up front, assists me in weather of this type.

Firm Footing Fundamental It is also important to have a secure stance. Often the ground becomes very skiddy and one can often slip as he attempts to execute the shot. Anything can result if you are unable to keep your balance and you do slip. Keep the spikes in your shoes long, replacing any that have worn down and/or are missing, keeping them clean of dirt and grass which can accumulate, widen your stance slightly, and shorten your backswing.

Rain can be tricky, though. If the fairway is soft, and the danger of the ball bouncing into the rough is eliminated, you will find that a bolder stroke will pay dividends. And if the greens are likewise soaked with moisture, remember that you can hit the ball right up to the hole where it will sit down fairly well. This brings to mind a phenomenon: The green might be extremely wet *and* also very fast. A little bit of water, not enough for soaking, and they will maintain their slickness, and greens that are hard and fast will remain that way. So be on your guard.

Once they do become heavy and sodden underneath the grass and there is a noticeable amount of water in sight, you should know that you will have to hit your putts firmly. Also, you must remember that the ball will not break as much when there's this much water on the green and therefore you can hit the ball firmer and straighter for the hole than you would normally.

Wet Weather Rules In wet weather, a knowledge of the rules is important, and a quick check of the allowances given in the section entitled "Casual Water" might be a pleasant surprise.

Two winners of the Masters tournament, Arnold Palmer and Jack Nicklaus, owe victories in this green-jacket classic to their being allowed to drop their golf balls otherwise mired in "moisture" out onto drier surface and make a more sensible approach shot to the pin. Casual Water is defined as ". . . any temporary accumulation of water which is visible before or after the player takes his stance and which is not a hazard of itself or is not in a water hazard. Snow and ice are 'casual water' unless otherwise determined by Local Rule."

The rules also cover conditions that affect putting: "On the putting green, or if such conditions intervene between a ball lying on the putting green and the hole, the player may lift the ball and place it without penalty in the nearest position to where it lay which affords maximum relief from these conditions, but not nearer the hole!"

THE COLD AND THE HEAT

Continuing with "weather" instead of "whether," our always playing "where the sun shines" is only a figment of speech. Besides wind and rain, those of us on the tournament trail play in extreme heat, almost bitter cold, in high, dry climate and in low, humid atmosphere. Each has to be handled differently.

Proper Clothing's the Answer When it is cold, it is essential the golfer stay warm but retain freedom of movement. This means no bulky sweaters or jackets. Here we can borrow some items from the skiers, namely, their thermal underwear. A woolen long sleeve shirt and a lightweight sweater or windbreaker is usually all that is necessary, except for a warm hat, of course. If need be, special winter golf gloves are available that are thin enough to retain the "feel" and just heavy enough to keep the fingers warm. Should you be wondering whether a warm golf ball travels farther than one that is cold, the answer is "Yes, it does." So, if you have to play in the cold, keep a spare golf ball or two warmed up ready for action.

Proper clothing is vital on hot days, too, such as those which took the starch out of everyone playing the United States PGA championship in Dallas in 1963. Light-colored slacks and short sleeve shirts will not attract as much heat, and the head should be protected by a hat or cap. Because the hands and arms will perspire, dry towels should be taken along, as well as some spare golf gloves. Salt tablets help, so don't refuse to take them.

When the air is close and humid, personal comfort may be asking too much. Golfers will only have to accept the conditions, slow down the pace a bit, and play it cool by not getting over-tired.

In the high altitudes where the air is thin, a man's ego gets a treat: His tee shots travel about 15-25 yards farther than they normally do when he's back home. But it raises havoc with club selection for approaches to the green. As long as you plan on this extra distance, you will quickly adjust to the using of a more-lofted club for a seeming far-away approach shot.

15

The Value of Lessons

The life of a teaching professional is extremely hard, frustrating, sometimes drab and painful, not often enough rewarding. Occasionally, fortunately, some pupil will diligently apply his instruction, practice until the swing is methodical and go on to win tournaments. But, generally, he has to take more than he gives, and that is just the opposite from what he would want to do.

Avoid Quickie Remedies The worst situation, I would think, would be to have a golfer with a lot of potential come up to him and say, "I've been playing ten years. Don't change the way I swing. Just correct my slice. That's all. And do it right away." To keep peace, the pro will have to give the person one of those quickie remedies which will certainly stop the slice, but which will, in no time, undoubtedly have the man hooking. The advice isn't what's pathetic; it is the fact that, had the man gone to the professional for lessons earlier in his career, he would have been able to build his game around a solid foundation, instead of being forced into finding temporary answers to problems that will pop up as long as he'll be playing golf.

Get yourself to a teaching professional as quickly as possible, tell him what your ambitions are, how much time you can devote to learning, and open your mind to what he will suggest. Do not

104

be afraid to open up. If you have a physical disability, so inform him. Most teachers will be able to guide you into developing an efficient swing around any such problem.

Learn to Learn   Listen carefully but avoid nodding yes to everything he says *unless you understand completely.* Many times the advice that is so clear on the practice tee gets jumbled up while out on the course, and instead of your game's improving, it retrogresses.

The value of communications can never be overestimated. Once you and the teacher are on the same beam, the instruction becomes permanent. Then, whenever your game sours, it is a relatively easy matter to find the error on the practice tee. Otherwise, to attempt to correct a fault by yourself would be foolhardy. Even the touring professionals are not able to diagnose their own game to this extent.

Many would-be golfers are too shy to ask for lessons and this is unfortunate, because they are by-passing an almost guaranteed short-cut to pleasurable golf. When someone says he has never taken a lesson in his life, that person is more to be pitied than envied.

When the lesson time is up, do not hasten to the course to try to put the instructor's tips into immediate use. Try to practice everything that was covered until you make the suggestions a part of your game that you can rely on. The best instruction in the world would otherwise be wasted.

The Pros No Exception   The type of lesson would depend on your ability, knowledge of the game and experience, of course. This means that no one, regardless of handicap, is beyond asking for a session with his teaching professional, if only to have someone competent watching while he swings. The fact that errors can creep into a person's game is universally known. Seldom does a tournament go by but one hears of a pro giving a fellow colleague —and competitor—a tip that helped him putt his way to a win, or to add twenty yards to his tee shots, or to improve his bunker play, or to get his grip in proper position. If the pros, themselves, need this scrutiny, what of the weekenders?

Make an effort to find a teaching professional, place yourself in his care, listen with an open mind, and then practice what *he* preaches.

16
The Importance of Practice

To ask the majority of amateurs to practice before they play is expecting too much. But this is more in tribute to the game's attractiveness than in censure of them. There might be more free time available, but there are also more activities to tend to other than golf, so, it isn't surprising that the golfer hies it to the first tee raring to go.

For this type I would suggest those exercise hints described in another chapter, but for the ambitious golfer, I do strongly urge regular practice sessions, and all of them with a definite purpose or intent.

Take a Plan to the Tee   Take to the practice area some particular problem you want to work on, and stay with it until you have it resolved to your satisfaction. If whatever is bothering you hasn't been overcome, get the assistance of your professional. Do not ask the advice of anyone else, like a friend or a bystander. This would do irreparable harm.

Do not take to the area just to hit golf balls. Follow a plan and aim for a target. As a warm-up for a tournament or a friendly round, start with the short irons and work up through the middle and long irons, the woods to the driver, then try to get in a session with the wedge approach shots and some putting. Do not overdo it if you are scheduled for an early tee off.

Under no circumstance should you practice when tired. Then the session will only add to the problems. Take plenty of time between hits and stay relaxed. Spend a lot of time on "type" shots, that is, the deliberate hook, slice, low or high ball.

Experiment and Improve Learn to play the wind shots, try hitting balls from tight lies with every club in the bag, discover the many uses of the wedge, learn how to hit them high or low with this valuable club and, when possible, practice those hilly lies.

The practice area is golf's real incubator. It is there that questions about the mechanics of the game are answered, experiments are proved or disproved, swings are grooved, and confidence restored.

17

Exercise Suggestions

The first of the practice hints is to suggest a few minutes daily to just grip and re-grip a golf club, to get accustomed to the right grip and also to retain "feel" for the club. This is especially beneficial to the high handicap golfer. Take the grip in your right hand and then in your left, then get both hands on the grip correctly, and give the club a little waggle. You do not need a full swing: Merely by gripping and re-gripping, getting a feel of the club for these few minutes daily, you will strengthen your hand muscles and also keep your hands, fingers, wrists and forearms in the right groove, ready for action on the weekend.

Swing a Weighted Club   The other tip is to swing a weighted club or, if one isn't available, use those weighted head covers that can slip over the head of your regular club. It is an excellent warm-up device, one that will slow your swing down a lot, and you soon develop rhythm as well as a slow, easy, efficient swing. You will strengthen not only the wrists, but all the golfing muscles which you use. In so doing, it will help you get the extra distance which is so necessary, anywhere.

Use a Full-Length Mirror   Then, too, there is that mirror, as large a one as possible. A full length mirror can help you check on any movement of the head: I advocate a steady head position throughout, because I believe that the head, next to the hands, is one of the foundations of a good swing. I like to see it remain in the same position from the time the club is started back until after you've hit the ball. Try to keep it steady. It should not be ruffled down or moved sideways; it should just remain in that fixed position and you should swing around it, so to speak. You can imagine your head nailed to something behind you and just swing around it accordingly.

Looking in the mirror will also give you an idea on whether you are actually gripping it correctly, that the grip you are using is holding the club in the correct plane, it can point out any swaying movement, any incorrect roll of the wrist, and whether you are lining up to the shot correctly. I vote for the mirror as one very important aid in getting to know a little bit more about the game—and the way you play it.

Golf Isometrics Work Fine   I will also vote in the affirmative for doing physical exercises, but caution against developing muscles not used in or needed by a good golf game. Now, for instance, swimming is not really a good exercise for golf, although we all know swimming is one of the greatest activities for exercising just about every muscle in the body. I would prefer golf isometrics, devices that strengthen the wrists, hands and fingers, and anything you can to keep the legs in shape and yourself in top physical condition. Any or all of the above will build up the proper golfing muscles and will improve your golf, I am certain, as long as you never do them to excess.

18
Equipment for Left-handers

I have often been asked if I designed my own clubs, and if the set I'm using was especially made for me. The answers to both are both yes and no. I do contribute ideas, along with the other golf professionals on the staff of the company I represent. But other suggestions are requested from and submitted by the home professional, as well. The ideas then are evaluated by a golf club engineer at the plant, wood and iron models are made up which include the important features of the design or designs selected by his department. These models are carefully checked by a committee composed of executives from manufacturing, engineering, sales and merchandising departments, and, after the model or models are selected, steel castings are made of the woods and forging dies set up for the irons.

The reason why I said yes and no to the question of whether my set was specially made for me is that my company does make up a set for my particular specifications, but in the making of a set of registered clubs today, so many steps are hand operations that almost all of them can be said to be hand-made, and if a set is not available that fits you properly, you can order a special set for yourself. Thus, you, too, can be outfitted to your own specifications.

Need Not Be Ashamed   No question about it. The equipment left-handed golfers can select from today is enough to make any portsider drool. This is by no means any special pitch for my own clubs that the Dunlop people make available to golfers on both sides of both oceans; it is merely a thankful note from someone who was born into the realization that it was not this simple just a short time ago. It wasn't too easy for me, but it was doubly hard for my parents who introduced me to golf, gave me hand-me-down clubs and taught me the solid fundamentals. Nowadays, you can purchase a set of perfectly matched clubs, clubs in the particular set that belong to each other in feel, swingweight, balance, just by walking in to see your own club professional, looking at his large inventory, check a few for length, lie and swingweight, and taking your pick. The left-hander still doesn't have the wide variety the right-hander has, of course, but the very fact that clubs are available, and in open stock, is just about the greatest news the left-hander can have. No longer does the southpaw have to play with 14 clubs that have 14 different flex points, grip sizes and over-all weight. And no longer is he so ashamed of the club he is using that he has to hit the ball quickly and jam the instrument back into the bag. If his clubs are of recent vintage, he is using a precision-built implement designed to hit a golf ball with as much perfection as his swing allows.

Today's clubs represent years of research and development on the part of the manufacturers who follow a proved formula in patterning the correct combination of head weight, head size, face progression, shaft deflections and wall thicknesses, grip size and club length and club lie that will fit the majority of golfers. And for those who want something a bit different from standard, the club makers have a special custom-tailoring department at your service.

Touring the Factory   In fact, a trip to the plant to watch the clubs being made is always fascinating. To start at the beginning, you might be taken to see hundreds upon hundreds of preformed persimmon "blanks" being aged before undergoing the operational steps that will transform them into shiny, durable woods. Or you might be shown the forging hammer exerting two to five thousand pounds of pressure on the round steel bar stock which is to become the gleaming, precisely built iron head. If fortunate, you might also see how shafts are made from steel rings, drawn by the most modern extremely powerful shaft roller compressors, or be shown the patented tubular shaft construction by bonding 501,000 strands of glass fibers to form an outer wall over a spiral inner wall. These fibers, in a semi-liquid state initially, are extruded over mandrels of the proper diameter prior to being oven cured and solidified. These new shafts provide a new measure of control and feel and represent the newest advancement in golf club design in today's manufacturing procedures. These tiny strands of fiber glass interact to generate a progressive build-up of power from the top down to the clubhead and are so located and arranged to provide the maximum efficiency in end use. The continuous taper of these thousands of tough glass fibers generates an uninterrupted power build-up through the whole length of the shaft, and will remain in their original condition even after many years of playing use.

The Wood Heads Are Formed   Here, briefly, is a description of how the heads for the woods are formed: After seasoning, the blanks are graded to determine the weight and density of each, then a machine saws away all unnecessary corners to make the blocks easier for insertion into semi-automatic turning machines. The actual forming of the head according to the specifications takes place in a special lathe where it is contoured in precise, unvarying conformity, guided by the steel-turning forms which produce the left or right hand models. Then comes the critical operation of drilling the hole in the neck of the head to accept the shaft. The care that must be given to this job should be obvious: The slightest deviation in aligning the hitting surface of the clubface with the center line of the shaft would put the entire club out of whack, and would mean a lessening in accuracy, feel and satisfaction. The head is next slugged with a pre-determined amount of lead poured into a hole drilled on the bottom or sole, and then put through a series of cutting or "routing" steps that will perfectly hold the face insert and the sole plate.

The insert is of material selected to provide an excellent hitting surface that will impart a good sense of feel and maximum distance when it contacts the ball. The sole plate has a direct bearing on the stability and durability of the wood club, by being

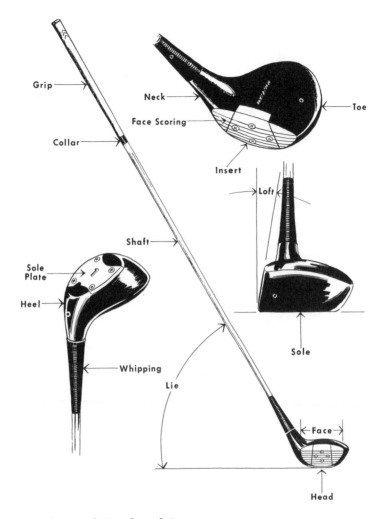

Nomenclature of Woods and Irons

An equipment phenomenon will have a golfer who is forced into using a strange set of clubs then play his finest round of the year. Or he can purchase an expensive new set that has everything but the same "feel" of his ancient ones. However, these are isolated situations. You will definitely perform in accordance to your tools—*provided* they fit you. The finest clubs in the world will do you no good if they are of the wrong length, or lie, or have the improper shaft for your swing, or even if the grip is of incorrect size.

You won't be alibiing if you try to determine whether your errors are a result of ill-fitting clubs. I shudder when I think of the few selections available to us left-handed golfers just a few years ago. In some areas there were none, and the enthusiast had to go at it from "the wrong side," using right-handed clubs. But today it is different. Club-making has become a scientific art, with precision assured by the guidance of a strict formula.

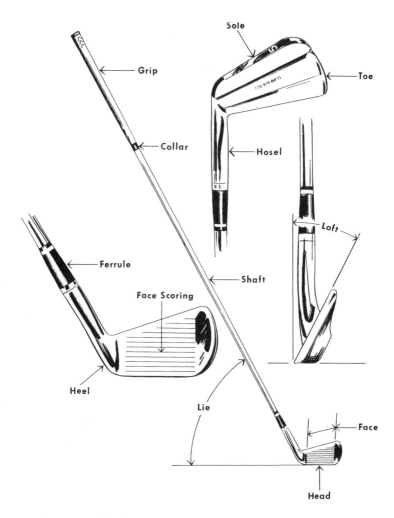

There is a built-in relationship between grip size and weight, shaft length and deflection, and clubhead size and weight. This "balance" or "swing-weight" produces the feel that gives you confidence when you reach for any particular club in any particular circumstance. Now the club of today, as fine an instrument as it is, is not so delicate that it won't withstand the punishment of repeated hits, yet it is such that adding any weight to either end, such as tape to repair loose whipping on the woods, or building up the grips, will change this balance.

Although individual shapes and sizes vary, most of our arms are of a length as to be approximately the same distance from the ground, the factor in determining correct length, and most of the standard sets of clubs fall within this length. Also, the manufacturers have successfully standardized the balance and the feel in each of the three most common shaft deflections (stiff, medium and flexible) so that a purchaser can generally be assured that the clubs he selects will deliver to the maximum of his skill. It is a great day for club buyers, especially the long-neglected left-handers.

proportioned to eliminate any stresses which can cause breakage. The sanding, shaping and finishing operations follow, and the final touch is the protective and beautifying coats of varnish, sealer and lacquer, plus a lot of shine-producing buffing. When the wood is fitted to its shaft, the end product is an instrument of beauty and playability.

The irons, too, undergo precise, constantly inspected treatment, and it is a more complicated implement than it appears to be. For one thing, the finish has to be able to withstand the highly corrosive fertilizers and other chemical colorings which not only tarnish a club but also rust and pit the metal. Too much of this can actually cause loss of weight, especially when such heads are polished and buffed from time to time to renew their original lustre. Even distortion can result.

Swing Weight and Total Weight High in the advancement in design of today's irons has to be the "feel" each club has, the result of pre-determining shaft and head weights to produce a club to a given and desirable swing weight. Swing weight is an arbitrary measurement indicating the distribution of the weight of the club. It is the proportion of the weight in the head compared to the shaft and the grip, and is measured on a logarithmic scale. The higher the swing weight, the heavier the club will "feel." It should not be confused with total weight, which is *actual* weight and which will differ with the clubs within the same set, especially in the irons which get heavier in actual weight as they go up in number. Swing weight also gives the club its balance, and any change, such as takes place if you build up the grips by yourself or if you try to repair a club with tape or if you lengthen or shorten the shaft, can be spotted rather easily by those who golf regularly.

The Iron Heads Are Forged The blade of the iron not only has to look good, it has to feel good, too. And this means it has to swing good. Today's irons feature a center of gravity that has been moved away from the heel to a spot nearer the actual center of the blade, thereby increasing power and accuracy. If the weight were concentrated too far out on the toe, "torque" will be produced, capable of opening and closing the clubhead during the downstroke, a condition commonly called "toe flutter." If the weight were to be nearer the heel, this would be an open invitation to the dreaded shank.

Also the modern day iron heads feature the center of gravity that has been moved downward or lower on the clubface, and the heads have been so designed that the hosel can accept the shaft with its center line in direct relationship to the point of impact. This, too, is a notable change.

Before production begins, all factors must be known and adhered to in every rigid respect. This means, for both woods and irons, each club's loft, lie, length, head weight, over-all weight, weight and wall structure of the shaft, its nature and amount of flexibility, the size and taper of the grip and its component parts, including cap texture. What is more, the irons will include nine or ten *different* heads in the set that must be matched to each other when produced. While no two are alike in size, loft, lie and weight, they all must be perfectly matched upon being finally assembled.

Each iron clubhead stems from a round steel bar stock, usually pre-cut into $7\frac{1}{2}$ inch slugs which are placed in heated furnaces to fill out the impression in the forging die where, under the two thousand to five thousand pounds pressure, it produces a head properly "set" for loft and lie, without scale. Control of weight is given as much attention at this point as at the finish. Immediately the heads are subjected to more pounding, this time by trimming presses exerting pressure of some two and one half tons. Under the trimming dies, which match the forging dies, the excess flash from the previous operation is removed and the pattern of the club can be seen; it has begun to take shape.

It is next prepared for the drilling of the hosel which, as with the woods, represents the most critical operation. It is the centerless grinder which brings the hosel to the proper size and taper, and when it is also ground perfectly smooth, it is ready for drilling on and by a multiple spindle drilling machine, an automatic operation which drills and reams the head to provide accurate alignment. In a following milling operation, the head is broached also to produce accurate surfaces to aid the stamping and face scoring steps which follow.

The lines on the clubface are what is known as "scoring" and to furnish the markings that meet with the USGA specifications calls for the utmost skill. The specific rule reads, in part: "Club faces shall not bear any lines, dots or other markings with sharp or rough edges, or any type of finish, made for the purpose of

putting additional spin on the ball . . . In general it is required
that the face of an iron club shall present a smooth, flat surface
on which a limited percentage of the area may be depressed by
markings . . . When the depressed area is in the form of grooves,
each groove may not be wider than approximately one thirty-
second of an inch, the angle between the flat surface of the club
face and the side of the groove may not be less than 135 degrees,
and the distance between grooves may not be less than three
times the width of the groove. . . ."

This operation is performed on a press supplying about 300
tons of pressure!

Several Shaft Deflections   Now a few words about the right
shaft for you. Normally, there are at least three different flexes
available in your pro shop or store; stiff, medium and flexible,
and it usually isn't too difficult to select the correct one. Your
strength, muscle tone, age, golf ability and swing habits are
among the characteristics which should be taken into account
before you select the one for you. A person who swings easily
might find that the flexible shaft provides just the right amount
of extra "help" he needs to get extra distance with his present
swing. The strong hitter would find this club too flexible and too
uncontrollable and would be better off by using a stiff shaft. The
medium, of course, will be for the "medium" person. Be aware,
though, of the in-between flexes that make a shaft a "medium-
stiff" or a "stiff-medium." Really.

It is not too difficult to tell if the shaft you are using is too
stiff: In time you'll find that your arms will begin to tire just
above the wrists, you will lose the use of the wrists and the club
will feel heavy and unbending. It'll then be time to switch to a
shaft with the medium flex. You will also know if the shaft is too
flexible by a lack of control and clubhead feel.

In purchasing a set of clubs, remember that it is the distance
your hands are from the ground that determines the length of
the shaft for you. Let your arms hang down naturally as you
stand fairly normally, in just a bit of a crouch. Grip the club you
are thinking of buying and assume your address position, then
look at the sole of the club. Or, better yet, have a competent
person check it for you. If it is fairly flat to the ground, with the
toe just slightly up, say about an eighth of an inch, then it would
have the proper "lie" for you. (The lie is that angle as measured

from the bottom of the club *back* to the shaft. The most carefully matched, finest balanced, most expensive set in the world will be of little value if the lie is not right for you.)

Extra length clubs are available, sometimes in open stock, but always on special order. Mine are three quarters of an inch longer than standard, or 43¾ inches for the driver and 39¼ inches for the 2-iron, the two clubs which are used to determine the corresponding or proportionate length of any set. Some golfers use drivers that are much longer than standard just for the purpose of generating more clubhead speed at impact and thus get more distance. This theory is true, but if the longer driver can't be handled, it won't do what it is supposed to, and you will be sacrificing not only accuracy but money, as well.

The majority of golfers can get along fine with medium shafts, a D1 to D4 swing weight, the prescribed lofts standardized by the manufacturers, and the standard size grip. But, since all balance and feel of the club is transmitted through the hands, the proper grip—for you—is important. You can select leather, rubber, composition and all-weather types. I have my own preference, naturally, but it may not be the one you like. I suggest you try them all, and decide for yourself. As for grip size, that is extremely important, because one that is too small will force you into gripping the club too tightly, taking away all feel, rhythm and control, while one that is too large will lighten the head and tend to induce an improper swing. Grip size is usually measured at a point two inches from the top. Because I have long fingers and because I was inclined to grip tightly, my grips are larger than normal.

Buying a Set of Clubs   The key to good golf is the club you are using, and today's golf club is a superbly tailored instrument. Now I am not suggesting you throw away your old clubs and run out to buy a new set. I know of a young club professional who fought his way up the amateur ranks into a club post by virtue of his ability to play excellent golf (as well as his good nature, his teaching talents and his business sense), but all that time he was using a set of store-bought clubs that had as many swing weights as there are days in the week. His newly acquired sponsor, horrified, quickly air-mailed to him the finest set possible just in time for his debut in a PGA co-sponsored tournament. Although perfectly matched, they didn't accompany him more than four holes of a practice round before he put in an S.O.S. to the manufacturer's agent, begging his old clubs back. And he got his wish. He then played the tournament proper with his mis-matched but familiar clubs and finished in a creditable, incredible tie for twentieth place. The reason? He was convinced his new set did not fit him or his swing—and he was right. However, and happily for sponsors, he has since been properly fitted, his old "trusted" clubs have been retired to the caddie house, and he is going to be a man to be reckoned with in the future.

Very often amateurs also hang onto clubs that likewise should have been retired. They give as reasons financial difficulties, which is all right, of course, preference for the old as compared to the new, which will be tough to prove and extremely simple to disprove, or superstition, they won a big championship with them. All of this, while understandable, is foolhardy, if the golfer has ambitions of ever improving his pleasure.

Today's clubs are easily the finest. If you use them, I've no doubt that you'll play your finest, too.

19

The Golf Ball Story

The center of attraction in any golf match is the golf ball. Even if you pay your money to follow your favorite at a tournament site, making him your particular center of attraction, what is *he* following? The golf ball. And some of us can become quite attached to one.

I gave thanks to a golf ball once. Well, more than once, really, but one was very memorable. It was on the 72nd hole of the 1963 British Open. Phil Rodgers and I both had taken the identical number of strokes up to the precise time we took our putters in hand and looked over our next shots. I charged mine a bit and went past the cup about 4 feet. Phil's birdie try, which could have won it for him, missed by two feet, then he almost missed his next. But, there he was already in with his par, and I needed my four footer to tie for the Open. When it disappeared, my affection for this little round white object grew and grew.

Many golfers find it difficult to select the right ball for them, and they'll want to know all about compression, cover hardness, type of center, depth and number of dimples, and the whys and wherefores of each. It is all extremely interesting, as are the actual manufacturing operations, some of which we'll try to describe.

What's Inside   The heart of the ball is its center, and through the years since the "modern type" golf ball was introduced, such substances as steel, fiber glass, pills, rubber, lead, silicone, water, blood, iodine, mercury, tapioca, dry ice, gelatin, arsenic and viscous pastes have been used in or as centers. It seems that both liquid and steel are most popular today.

The centers are then encased in a core that is usually highly resilient, over which pre-stretched, highly taut windings are applied, building up a powerful reservoir of energy. The windings might well hold the secret to the golf ball's consistency and compression, both, and, so important is it, all manufacturers pay careful attention to the way they are applied. Some manufacturers put the winding on in one operation, others in two; but it has been said that this tension builds up enough energy in the thread to lift a 150 pound man two feet off the ground. The pressure on the center builds up to about 2,500 pounds per square inch! Tests are continuously being made to indicate trueness, consistency and impetus ratings of the windings.

Now the ball is ready to be covered with material that is more resilient, more durable, and yet, has more feel than ever before. Formerly the cover that was too thin, as was once offered by the makers to impart a good "click" when hit, turned out to be quite fragile, also. When at the mercy of the high handicapper, the ball would not last too far beyond the third or fourth hole. It is different with today's models, most of which are made from balata, the milky juice of the West Indian balata tree which dries to form a hard, elastic gum covering.

The Cover Has Dimples   Two halves or "hemispheres," perfectly smooth, are placed over the elastic wound center and core of the ball and inserted in special ovens under thousands of pounds of pressure. While this operation adheres the two halves together, it also applies the dimples to the ball. These indentations, usually numbering 336, actually affect the flight of the ball. Their number, size and depth are influential aerodynamically speaking because the ball, when hit, rotates at a rate of 4,000 to 5,000 revolutions per minute. The back-spinning rotation causes air to pile under the ball while sucking it away from the top. This creates a pressure underneath and a vacuum-like reaction above, similar to the principle which gets and keeps the airplanes aloft. Any change in the dimples would change the pattern of trajectory to the ball.

What's on Top Counts   But perhaps the most noteworthy improvement, at least it is the most obvious, is the gleaming white finish, the result of polyurethane paint. The ball is now whiter to start with (in the manufacturing process) and aided by several coats of primer and finish paints, plus a clear coat to lock all this in, it stays white, round after round. One doesn't have to go too far back to recall how the golf balls, hoarded over the winter months, turned to a yellowish tint when they were taken out of storage in spring. Or to the days when the white paint of the golf ball would mar the hitting surface of the golf club. Or when the leather of the ball pocket of the golf bag discolored even new balls a dull, used-looking shade. Today's golf balls not only retain their whiteness, they also show less wear and tear compared to those produced only a few years ago.

The USGA and the R & A   More than any other piece of equipment, the golf ball is constantly being subjected to tests and investigations. The main reason, of course, is the ruling of the United States Golf Association which imposes a velocity limitation on the distance the golf ball used in tournaments in America and in countries under the jurisdiction of the USGA. This Rule states: ". . . The velocity of the ball shall be not greater than 250 feet per second when measured on the USGA's apparatus; the temperature of the ball when so tested shall be 75 degrees Fahrenheit: a maximum tolerance of 2 percent will be allowed on any ball in such velocity test." The tolerance pushes the maximum speed to 255 feet per second.

There are two other USGA restrictions which affect the distance and flight of the American golf ball, and that is weight, 1.62 ounces *maximum,* and size 1.68 inches *minimum.* (Under the Royal and Ancient rules, there is no velocity restriction at present; the weight is the same but the smaller size, at 1.62 inches, is the notable difference.)

But velocity, weight and size are the only stipulations the USGA imposes on the manufacturers. This means that those who make the golf balls have to concentrate elsewhere to produce a ball that gives a good click when hit, that stays whiter hole after hole, one that lasts longer, and one that offers continued trueness in flight, both in the air and on the ground. If they were to make a ball that was heavier than allowed, it would travel farther, which is attractive, but it would be illegal. And if they produced a ball that was smaller in size, it also would travel farther, but it, too, would be illegal. So, with only good golf balls to choose from, which, then, is the correct ball for you?

The Compression Factor   The easiest way to find out which is the right ball for you is to try different ones and make your selection from feel and distance. It is awfully difficult and too risky to tell someone else what ball he should be using, because of the many factors that should be considered. For example, the so-called high compression golf balls are built to go far *if hit a solid blow.* They require a hit from a golfer whose swing is grooved and whose maximum acceleration is reached at impact. If a soft hitter were to play the same ball, the energy that is inside, waiting to be released by a big hit, would actually work against him. The ball would not flatten out at impact and regain original shape as it speeds far down the fairway. The soft swinger, then, would get more yardage by using a ball with a lower compression rating, a "softer" ball that would react to his force more efficiently.

In general terms, then, compression relates to the hardness of the ball, and the harder (higher compression) the ball, the less "give" it has and the more force is needed to release the energy stored within the ball. The ultimate distance will be in relation to compression, velocity of the clubhead and the efficiency of the swing. When the ball of the golfer's choice, high, medium or low compression, reacts completely and correctly to the force of his swing, hard, medium or soft, the result should in each respective instance be maximum distance and maximum control.

One last note of caution (or confusion?): Maximum distance and maximum control are dependent in large part on the efficiency of the swing. You must consistently get the clubhead into the ball on the proper plane, in the correct arc and at the proper speed. Because there is a wide variation in these factors among golfers, it is difficult to fit a player to a ball of a specific compression rating. Even to observe a person's swing doesn't always help. A golfer who appears to swing hard may be hitting with a lot of body, while a lazy-type hitter might have extremely fast hands. The tendency is to recommend a high compression ball to the hard hitter, but do not be fooled by a hard swing that is inefficient or a smooth, slow swing that is perfectly grooved.

You still don't know which ball is right for you? I play the one I'm using because it is most consistent from tee to cup.

20

Take Care of Your Property

Ground Chemicals Can Corrode The purchase of a set of matched woods and irons, not to overlook the bag and accessories, shoes and apparel, represents a sizable outlay of money. While the equipment of today is the finest ever offered, in precision and balance as well as in durability, it still needs some attention to keep it in tip-top shape. Regular, if only minimal, care is needed, not only to keep the iron heads gleaming and the woods sparkling, but also to protect the clubs from the corrosive chemicals now in use on fairways and greens.

When golf was first gaining in popularity, it was played on natural meadows, with natural fertilizers, if any. Today, to landscape the holes and keep the fairways lush and green, they are treated with corrosive chemicals which, while serving the purpose, could also rust and pit the metal of shafts and iron heads. If left unchecked, even for a short period of time, it could even affect the weight and balance of the clubs.

To restore the piano-top luster on the woods, apply a coat of furniture polish that also contains ingredients that will remove marks or stains, and follow with a good brushing with a soft cloth. Keep the woods protected with head covers, otherwise they will rub against each other while in the bag, scratching them perhaps beyond repair. Should the head covers get wet, remove them immediately upon completion of the round and dry them thoroughly before re-using them.

If your wood club is reinforced with neck whipping, keep it intact. Should this thread break, have your club re-wound, *with thread*. Do not use tape in a do-it-yourself attempt at repair: It is a fact that an additional ⅛ ounce to the clubhead can change the swingweight of the club one point!

The woods today are stronger and better looking than those of yester-year, but they must be given some care if you expect them to play and appear their best.

Common Sense Cleaning Tips   The irons, too, have undergone some changes from as recently as ten years ago, but the reasons for and the methods of keeping them clean remain the same: You can't play your best with clubs that are clogged with dirt or grass. Not only will the balance be affected, but the ball will react abnormally when hit. You will control the shot much better when you keep the clubface free of dirt. All that is needed, upon completion of the round, is a soaking in a soap and water solution, followed by a rinse and a wipe. That is all. Do not use any harsh brushes, steel wool or abrasives, or you will cut through the nickel-chrome plating, thus adding to the problem by ruining the club's appearance *and* balance. During play you can scrape, but gingerly, any impediment in the face scoring (lines) with the pointed end of a tee, or you might prefer to use a wet towel. Remember the twofold objectives: to play better, and to better protect your investment.

But there's another end of the club to consider—the top. The grips are noticeably improved, yet, through constant use or abuse, they may become frayed or worn. Resist the impulse to "save money" by building them up with some application of tape: The addition of ¹⁄₃₂ of an inch to the grip reduces the swingweight by at least one point.

Next, or rather, in between, there is the shaft. Be careful how you pack your clubs in your car. It does them no good if they are the first to go into the trunk, under heavy luggage. And don't bang your clubs into the ground in disgust. In either case the shafts more than likely will bend, ruining the club's balance and precision.

Pay Special Attention to Shoes   Also give some care to your golf shoes. They carry most of the weight, so make certain they fit and feel as comfortably at the end of the round as they did at the outset. Treat them with a good leather conditioner and use shoe trees to maintain their shape. Remove grass and dirt from the spikes and soles before placing them in your locker, carry-all bag or car trunk. The spikes are a functional attachment to help you keep your balance while executing the shot: Check periodically for any that might be loose or missing. I would suggest you have at least two good pair of shoes.

Your golf bag must be of ample size to contain the number of clubs you find necessary to use. Too often a small bag is purchased and the golfer then has to jam his full complement of clubs into too small a space, thus raising havoc with the grips and endangering the shafts, as well. If your bag is of leather, treat it twice a year with the good leather conditioner you have used on your golf shoes. This will prevent its cracking and will protect it against excessive wear while adding to its looks. Replace the strap when there is evidence of wear and avoid the inconvenience of a possible strap break in the middle of a round. Also check the condition of the zippers and avoid the expense of losing costly items you might have stored inside the pockets. Do not allow anyone to sit on the bag. This will destroy the rings that give it its shape and strength.

A Life-Time Investment   Taking everything into consideration, the initial cost of top grade golf equipment is rather high, but with little care the investment can be one that lasts a lifetime. When you buy the best and protect it, you will play better, receive more for your money, look better, and enjoy the game to the fullest.

5/13